CHRIST: THE DARK YEARS

CHRIST: THE DARK YEARS

Brian D. Diederich

Dominion House Press
2009

Historical Edition

Dominion House Press

ISBN
978-0-578-00913-1

"The greatest blasphemy of all is to stand in Judgment of a person be they; friend or foe, rich or poor, worker, slacker, believer, learner, soldier, doctor, artist, writer, sinner, minister, a person filled with love, a person with hate, for we are all meaningless when compared to gods greatness."

Father Heime Grace

CONTENTS

CHRIST: THE DARK YEARS INTRO

The books of old not censored by the high priest of the Pharisees do tell of the dark years of Jesus Christ the years of agony, dread, lust, brutality and death.

The lost books reveal what Jesus did during the years we previously had no record. The Bible details the ministry of Jesus and makes only a couple of references to his youth. It mentions the events surrounding his birth and a story of Jesus as a young boy intimidating the High Priests, because of his intimacy with God, his wisdom, and his knowledge of the scripture. "And all who heard him were astonished at his understanding and answers."(Luke 2:47) Jesus soon found that all of the so called High Priests did not hold the key to the meaning of human existence. The child of God incarnate felt a need to really experience life in the flesh, so he left his cloistered life, and ventured alone, full-fledged into the quagmire of human filth and existence.

During these years, Christ first wandered south into Egypt, the land of the dead and godless. Here, he witnessed worshipers of death and read the Egyptians' Book of the Dead. They taught Jesus to heal by showing him parts of the dead and how the body worked. He also met a Grand Daughter of the Great Pharaoh Cleopatra here.

The Christ child then went to Asia Minor and drank from the poppy-tea of the great oracles he encountered. He found that this powder made Him stop hurting more than anything else. He decided to move on rather than become a slave to the substance. This whole journey was a preparation for Jesus when Satan was to test his will again.

Later, Christ went farther East. He brought many ideas to India with Him. The sages instantly saw that Jesus was a wise man who had a direct linkup to the ultimate stage of reality. The Sages exchanged ideas of reincarnation, the levels of reality, and the oneness of existence.

Once, when Jesus was meditating in the desert, a strange cactus-looking plant suddenly sprang from the earth. It was one that he had never seen in that area of Asia Minor. A strange desire came to Jesus to partake of the fruits of this plant, and He finally succumbed to it.

Within minutes of eating it, strange metamorphic transformations began to overtake Him. He felt his body start to shrink, and He could hear His bones crack and break under the force of the transformation. He could feel His body being stretched in all positions until finally when He stretched out His arms one final time, they had become wings, and he could feel the full force of the wind beneath Him. The lord Jesus Christ flapped His wings and flew up into the sky.

Jesus Christ incarnate, creator of heaven and earth was a Hawk. His wings carried him across the great ocean and Jesus hunted fish along the way. And when he finally crossed the great ocean, He came upon what we know as Americas. It was here that He came upon the mystic force that brought him there, a gang of Navajo Indians engaging in a peyote ceremony. The constraints of humanity were purged and in this He truly became as one with God and in full realization of His omnipotence and will.

The child of God entered the Underworld and the Valley of Death. In the Underworld, the Christ child had to try to bring fallen angels back to the domain of benevolence. In the Valley of death he was confronted by evil demons and misplaced spirits.

2

In addition to these events, Jesus was greatly inspired by the Three Wise Men and the women in his life. He sometimes traveled and studied with the three wise men, each of whom had a different vision of how he should achieve his mission on earth. Mary Magdalene, and Mary his mother taught Jesus love but it was Joanna that taught him to treat every person with respect because everyone is a part of God.

He traveled to Africa three times, as well as Babylon, India, and Asia. He was influenced by the people he came into contact with, and likewise, influenced them and their religions. He also indirectly influenced the natives of the Americas. The lesser-known disciples as well as religious sects had a greater role in his life than most people are led to believe

Jesus studied the science and magic of his day. The Child of God struggled with his own humanity and the ideas of early religious sects. Christ often challenged sexism and other unjust causes.

Early in life, Jesus tried to negotiate with leaders of the Western Oppressors. He then led an insurgency against the Romans, but many followers died in vain. Finally, he decided to begin his ministry and spread his message of peace through the martyrdom of his followers.

Along his path to truth, Jesus Journeys to distant lands and exchanging ideas, tries to end the Roman occupation of Israel, and had children. Further, he joined secret societies and mingled with cults. Also, he had the great mission sent down from god, of educating the masses to the light of truth..

The Child of God said do not fear ghosts for they are in heaven and you are only receiving their signal. Love opens the gate so that you can perceive visions from the dead. Children know this love but many lose touch of it. You cannot fully receive the message from another persons' soul and that is why ghosts do not appear solid except in dreams. "Before I formed you in the womb, I knew you before you were born" (JER 1:5). The soul of a person is the part that is in heaven before, during, and after their body lives in this world. Our flesh is a window that allows our soul in heaven to experience the carnal desires of the flesh. He called the signal our Spirit or Shadow. Jesus said that those who shut out this signal do not hear their inner voice, so they will not know themselves and therefore cannot know love of another and will deny God.

His task on earth was as dangerous as it was enormous. He was the first prophet to fight racism, sexism, nationalism, and occupation of invading armies. Furthermore, the mission of Jesus included reminding people of the oneness of existence, to reveal the law handed down by Moses, and to bring some fallen angels back into the army of God and, finally, to give man a path to redemption. God told his child of love that he was made fully human so that he could enjoy mortal experiences. Because he was given a free will, the messiah had to make his own choices, and decide on his own, how to achieve his purpose in life. God also gave him an unusual amount of compassion, intelligence, and a large memory of past lives. The forces of evil had a long time to take over the psyche of mankind, and there would be many to stand in his path and to try to hide his true word.

The complete story of the life of Jesus has recently been translated directly from manuscripts that were previously lost. Events and teachings that have been sequestered for centuries are revealed in this testament. The following is the true story of the dark years of Jesus Christ.

A BLESSED BABY

The parents of the newborn child were poor people, belonging by birth to a family of noted piety, who praised the name of the Creator and thanked him for the ills with which he saw fit to provide them despite their heritage. Angels visited Joseph and Mary and told them that they were being blessed by God with his own offspring in the flesh, as a reward for not turning aside from the way of truth. Brahmins, Lamas and wise men arrived from many distant lands to offer assistance in heralding in the life of this child of God that was foretold in the ancient writings and announced by the alignment of stars.

Many great Magi from the East "fell down and worshiped Him when he was a babe" (matt 2:11). Although many wise people came to visit Jesus three of them brought gifts and are mentioned in the bible. The three wise men who brought gifts were Balthazar, Gasper, and Melcher. They each came to Jesus and praised him as the new king. Balthazar represented nobility from Arabia, Casper was royalty from India, and Melcher was a great King in Persia. There are Ancient stories about kings bearing gifts to a savior so their appearance was just another sign that Jesus was the son of God. All three of them followed and studied the stars and other sciences. They each believed that the westerners should be converted to monotheism, but they disagreed on how. They also disagreed on what should be done about the influence Rome had on the people.

The First Miracle of Jesus was when he spoke as an infant to his mother Mary and said, "I am a servant of God." All the people present were amazed and astonished. They all agreed to keep this miracle a secret. Jesus spoke often as a child and amazed many. When he was still an infant, he told his family to go to Egypt to escape the massacre of King Herod's soldiers.

King Herod was having his men gather all children under the age of two. Stories existed about putting infants into an orphanage which was nothing more than a concentration camp where babies were left to starve. The king's men eventually slaughtered all innocents that remained in Bethlehem. Joseph decided to melt away rather than register Jesus with the monarchy. Jesus and his family along with many from his town became refugees in Egypt.

In Egypt, Joseph and Mary sent him to nursery school before they realized that he needed advanced tutoring rather than regular school. One day at school, he and the other children were playing with clay. Jesus sculpted twelve Sparrows, one of which was not perfect. He told his brother to watch as he released the sparrows, and they flew away. The one that was not formed perfectly flew a little slower than the others. Jesus said, "This is how god has made the world, all sculpted from the same earth, but some different than others" His brother and the other children were in awe of Jesus. They had all seen many magicians, but had never seen one perform something like this. Since only children witnessed this event, the adults in the village didn't take notice of Jesus and his special talents.

After a few years in Egypt, it became clear that Jesus was brilliant, and Philo took him as a pupil and was confounded at how quickly he mastered all the sciences, including medicine. He also knew all the tricks that magicians might perform. His first advanced teacher, Philo, was confounded that he could read and speak Greek and other languages fluently by the time he was only seven. Jesus showed that as a boy he was already a thinker and not interested in sports. He did enjoy playing war and finding sweet fruits in the wild with other boys.

A few years later, an older boy started picking on Jesus. He allowed this to happen for many days until one day when the boy came running toward him with raised fists. With his glare, Christ stopped the boy in his tracks, and the boy fell to the ground dead. The adults and townspeople started to gather and took the boy home to his bed. Jesus was very distressed about the commotion that he caused. Jesus was able to run in the house unnoticed by the adults and touched the boy as he lay on his bead. The boy awakened, and the adults in the room were amazed that Jesus performed such a miracle.

Some in the town were alarmed and called Jesus a sorcerer. A crowd began to gather and people started to protest what Jesus had done. The ones that were most vocal were suddenly struck blind, began to wander in different directions, and were never heard from again. Joseph decided to move his family away from the controversy. In fact, there were many times the family had to move. These moves continued until Jesus was sent to Asia to study with one of the wise men who visited him in his manger.

This was the first of three journeys to Egypt for Jesus. At age nine, Jesus and his family secretly returned to Jerusalem. After a second trip to Africa he traveled to Persia, India, and Asia. A goal of his Journey was to meet Doctors in Africa, Monks in Golan, Brahmins in India, and Buddha's in Asia. He knew he wanted to visit all the great houses of God if he could. His goal was to study the Divine Word and what mankind understood about the physical world. He was also interested in how the politics of the world worked for he knew that the patterns of early civilizations are repeated throughout history.

Jesus always remembered what his father in heaven said to him; "I am handing over my kingdom on earth to you. You must explain to the earthlings that I am one and all at the same time so that when I send you a second time they will be ready to enter my realm." He also always remembered his dedicated servants who promised to return one day and help him fulfill his mission.

THE WISE MEN RETURN

As a child, Jesus stirred up much trouble by asking questions and testing his magical skills. He wanted to become an artist when he grew up, but his parents wanted him to become a man of the cloth, so a letter was sent to his godfathers, the wise men, requesting that they take Jesus with them to study abroad as they had offered to do ten years earlier, when they met Mary and Joseph. Each of these three Zoraters had a different vision of how Jesus should convert the west to the ways of the true god.

Most western stories say the number of wise men was three because three gifts were presented to Jesus on the night of his birth, but there were actually twelve wise men. There was one Magi from each of the twelve known races, who visited Jesus during his infant years. Historians have gathered a collective knowledge of the three wise men that brought gifts to Jesus when he was in the manger.

The names of the three wise men bearing gifts were Balthazar, Casper, and Melcher. They each came to Jesus and called him the new king. They came from the East representing three of the worlds known races. Balthazar was from a royal family in Arabia, Casper was a prince of India, and Melcher was nobility of Persia. There are Old Testament prophecies about kings bearing gifts to a savior, so their appearance was just another sign that Jesus was the son of god. They were all Brahman who followed and studied the stars and other sciences. All three wise men believed that the westerners should be converted but they disagreed on how and what else should be done about the influence Rome had on the people.

The Three Magi each gave Jesus a different gift on the day of his birth. Balthazar was a handsome man, with a dark complexion, and thick beard. The myrrh that he gave to Jesus was a gift given to Egyptian kings to take with them to the afterlife. Balthazar had early premonitions about the death of the Son of God. Casper was young, beardless, and had a reddish complexion. Young Casper approached Jesus with enthusiasm and gave incense to Christ. The incense was from Afghanistan and had a strong fragrance. It was said that this incense brought all who inhaled it closer to god. Melcher was an old man, with white hair and a long beard. He slowly approached Jesus and offered gold to the Christ child as Homage to the Divinity of Jesus. These three men were all Magi, or Wise Men.

Each of the three wise men had different ideas about how to resolve the problem of westerners occupying the Middle Eastern nations. Balthazar believed that by talking to the Romans and recognizing their needs that a solution could be found where they might move their armies elsewhere. Casper, however, often argued that there was no way to appease the Romans. Casper told Jesus that the Romans plundered Persia for centuries to sustain their Power, thirst for treasure, and influence in the world. Casper supported the insurgency against the westerners who brought only pain, suffering, and idol worship to their lands. Melcher agreed that no one could convince the Romans that they were better off withdrawing their armies because their pride would not allow them to cut and run and admit defeat. However, Melcher said that the Romans could one day be converted to believe in One God and the books of Moses if given the proper inspiration. All three men believed that this conversion was possible if there was a great leader that could spread information and inspire the masses. All three maji were excited to help educate Jesus so that he could one day lead the revolution as they envisioned it.

Balthazar was the keeper of the sacred chart on which the early Egyptians wrote down what would happen to man in the end days. He told Jesus that he must travel often to Africa because although this is where all men come from, it is also where all men will exploit and be indifferent to in the future. Balthazar had big bulging eyes and carried a look on his face that showed he was always expecting something. He told his scribes this was because he always looked forward to the success of his prodigy Jesus. This wise man educated the Lamb of God and treated him like a son. Balthazar always had a smile and something nice to say about people he talked to. Most of his days were spent advising kings and those who sought out his seemingly infinite wisdom.

Casper was a very wise also, but he believed in fighting any enemies of knowledge rather than trying to change their minds. He later helped fund an insurgency against the Romans and became its spiritual leader. He sold his incense to fund this guerilla revolution and often smoked with those who believed as he did that only through the use of violence could the Romans be turned away. One day he laid his thick, ruddy hand on the shoulder of Jesus and said "follow the words of the testament which says, an eye for an eye, until every westerner is driven out of our lands". The followers of Casper claimed that those who did not convert to the testament of Moses should die by the sword. At first Jesus was attracted to the radical and violent ideas of Casper, but later in life, he rejects this course of action. In the end, Jesus started a non-violent resistance that uses martyrs to convert the Westerners by showing how a strong faith cannot be broken.

Melcher was a great wizard who had knowledge about the stars and tricks that he wanted Jesus to learn. He expected Jesus to live a long life and pass these discoveries on to the human race so that they could one day understand the concept of God. He could reach in his bag and bring out many lighted stars. He told young Jesus that he captured these stars from the heavens and put them in his bag. Jesus learned this trick and all the magic that Balthazar could show him. They learned ways to make fire and ways to make ice. They learned ways to make steam, and smoke and they used this to amaze the people. Melcher told Jesus to not be too rigid or too flimsy in his thoughts. Melcher had a fragile voice that trembled more than his hands. He told Jesus to pass the secrets of the ancients on to the people. He said, "let them know that through numbers and knowledge they will become closer to God and when they have enough knowledge, they will be able to comprehend his omnipotence." Jesus promised Melcher that he would be flexible about how to carry on his work, and that he would fight ignorance and help make new discoveries acceptable to the masses.

The Magi were a priestly class of people who ascended to power in ancient Persia which would one day be called Iran. Their religion, Zoroastrianism, was founded around the 6th century BC by a man named Zoroaster. The Magi were held in awe as highly learned alchemists, astrologist, and scholars who could interpret dreams and even control demons. They had a great knowledge of the stars and had charts of each stars movement over the years dating back to antiquity.

Each of the Magi lived over one hundred years and they all outlived Jesus. They all lived to see Christianity take root throughout the Roman Empire and were pleased with what Jesus had taught for mankind. The remains of the wise men were brought to Constantinople, which is present day Istanbul, by Helena, mother of the fourth century Roman emperor Constantine. Later their remains were moved to Milan and finally to Germany. A cathedral for the relics was built in Cologne, where they remain to this day. Legend says that the ghost of Casper still visits the good children of the world around Christmas time.

The wise men taught Jesus to use the right amount of opium so that his heart was almost stopped, and he could meditate in peace and harmony. When he was crucified, this helped him appear dead to the Roman Soldiers. The Super-Godchild met with all three wise men later in life. Each of them gave Jesus wisdom and power. Also each of the wise men took Jesus on a separate journey. He traveled with one to Africa, one to Babylon, and one to Asia.

EAST OF EDEN

The wise men were summoned by Mary and Joseph after Angels told them to send Jesus somewhere safe from the armies of the west. It was the magi Balthazar, who returned to take the Christ child on a Journey where they went East of Eden. First, they crossed the Nile into Egypt. They kept moving through the lands of the dead until they were East of Eden. Jesus was introduced to many Queens during their travels through Africa. His favorite damsel in Africa was a princess that was a Grand daughter of Cleopatra the Great. Also during this journey, Balthazar traded secrets about healing and the dead with Jesus and Egyptian Priests.

Ancient Egyptian doctors were the first physicians to study the human body in a scientific way. They showed The Christ how to set broken bones, care for wounds, and treat many illnesses in ways that were not revived until after the dark ages. The Lord of Benevolence witnessed these doctors cutting the sexual desires out of women and when he protested they became offended. This practice is still practiced in Northern Africa to this day by those who want to subjugate women.

Jesus performed many other similar experiments on Egyptian slaves to study the human body. He learned how to extract every organ from the human body as it was part of early Egyptian death rituals. In these rituals he experienced firsthand the practice of fornicating with the dead. He would stick his hands into a body and grab a part and try to figure out what it did. Blood was meaningless to the Egyptian priests, and at the end of the day, they would be in puddles of blood and immune to the stench of death. Jesus knew these people needed help and vowed to find out what was wrong with the world.

The Egyptians showed Jesus how to perform magnetic levitation. They also showed him how to magnify the magnetic field of the earth locally to control weather. A Priest in Egypt taught Jesus how to read a persons mind by looking deep into their eyes while making gestures that cause a person to reveal their thoughts. These Priest also had his scribes reveal all the secrets of astrology, the pyramids, and ancient visitors from heaven to the young Messiah.

Cleopatra lived in Egypt 30 years before Jesus was born. In an attempt to end the hatred some men had of women, Cleopatra gave all her power to the Secret Brotherhood there. This was a mistake because the brotherhood usurped her power and spread false tales about her after her death. It took centuries for women to regain their place in society.

Cleopatra's favorite son Ptolemy, ruled a kingdom in Syria, but he is known more for the fact that Jesus fell in love with his daughter while in Egypt. As soon as Jesus looked into the eyes of Cleopatra's Grand daughter, he loved her and would call her Mary.

Jesus and Mary had three children together. One son could not speak or see, another was hidden away by the brotherhood, and became the first secret leader of the world. Finally they had their only daughter, Sarah, and she was hidden away, so that she could be educated in a safe environment. After having these children, Jesus knew he needed to explore humanity more, and told his love that he would venture on alone, and would be with her again in the future.

At this time, Jesus infiltrated the Secret Brotherhood during a death cult meeting. This brotherhood guarded the river of knowledge that God passed down to the ancient races long before books were written. While there, he passed through seven degrees of initiation. The highest deacon stood at the altar with 13 swordsmen at his side. The deacon arose and said, "I place all that is wrong with the world on your shoulders. You alone must carry for god all the troubles and guilt of all mankind for centuries. Open the gateway between this realm and the infinite realities." At that instant, a voice that shook the desert floor said, "This is The Christ"; and every living creature for miles around said, "Praise Jesus."

Then he went south into the deepest, darkest jungle where he came upon people with many strange rituals, and many strange gods. He saw cannibalism here; the people would hack the heads off the bodies of those killed in combat and drink the blood from their skulls. Then, they would eat the flesh from their bones. During this procession, a strange metamorphic transformation would take place. The cannibals would always experience a euphoric surge as if they were enveloping the spirit from the flesh they consumed. That is why Jesus has us eat bread and drink wine; it is a representative cannibalistic ritual of the body of Christ. By eating his flesh and drinking his blood, we may become him.

\Death and disease were meaningless here and Jesus partook of the great killing sprees. Tribes would meet in the killing fields where they would fight until no man was left standing. Blood was in ponds and bodies littered the ground for miles. The carnivorous inhabitants eating raw flesh were his only companions that summer. The people here ate brains of the conquered to become one with their enemy and usurp their power and strength. The brains were the favorite part for some of these tribes and the child of peace did all he could to stop the mayhem while he was there. For a time, Jesus ran with packs of orphans and runaways so that he could experience the quagmire of human pain, filth, and existence.

He learned to love the dead as much as the living, and death as much as life. The power and adrenalin of killing and maiming made him feel alive. This was an aspect of the human psyche Christ would have a hard time overcoming.

Then, Jesus rejoined Balthazar and they traveled further. Balthazar told Jesus that he had a vision and knew that one day the forces of Commerce would fight the religious forces. "Your followers will have the best weapons and have faith in you but they will have to fight those within their own ranks who let idealism win over realism. There will be forces of commerce and forces of religion and the forces will fight each other. There will be three one thousand year periods of darkness in the East and the West. Also, children will be discarded with no remorse. This is what will become of the children of this land."

The Christ child and his mentor Balthazar traveled deeper into Africa where he met many strange tribes with customs he had never observed. Many people in this part of the world became sick from a rare disease which caused them to start bleeding from their eyes until their skin swelled with blood. Jesus said unto them that "your children's children will be left to fight each other as disease runs rampant. The powers of darkness will control the medicinal cures and eventually, their own greed will bring about the demise of their own people."

One day an older Brahman came down from Mount Kilimanjaro after meditating for six solid months. He told Jesus of the message he had heard: "Judge not your brother and treat others as if God's Judgment will come tomorrow."

Here Jesus had many followers. Girls would camp outside of his compound all night just to get a look at him. Entire tribes would leave their villages to follow him for months. Fathers would offer their sons as servants and their daughters as brides to Jesus.

Although Balthazar told Jesus to avoid military conflicts, he and Jesus often discussed armies and wars. They talked about finding recruits among the orphanages set up in camps for displaced tribes. "You can recruit these children while they are young and march them back to Jerusalem to fight the Romans." Jesus was concerned that too many would die of thirst while crossing the great desert and decided not to do this. Balthazar thought they would just be raped or sold to slave traders if he left them. The records of how this discussion was resolved are lost to antiquity. Also missing is mention of how Jesus made his way back to Jerusalem, where he met up with Casper, who took him to stay with the Esseans on their way to Babylon.

GUEST OF THE ESSEANS

As a youth, Jesus was already hanging out with radical teenagers who, were determined to drive foreign troops out of their land. So, when Casper visited with Mary and Joseph for tea in their humble living room and talked about taking young Jesus to far away lands, they saw this as a great educational opportunity for their son. Casper told them he would take Jesus far from soldiers and teach him some different philosophies. This made them glad to let him go, so Jesus and Casper set out on their Journey.

Casper first had Jesus stay with the Esseans who lived along the Dead Sea and in the wilderness between Jerusalem and Babylon. Officially, Jesus was a guest of the Esseans who were good hosts, but he actually served as one of their monks. He gained many followers for the sect but over time began to question their beliefs and most of the customs that conflicted with his lifestyle.

The Esseans are one of three leading Jewish sects that flourished for two hundred years before Christ's lifetime. The other two sects are the Pharisees and the Sadducees, whom he also visited. These two sects had greater numbers than the Esseans. He visited the Esseans because of their hospitality and cooperative way of living, not because of their numbers. The Esseans often took a vow of chastity, only relenting themselves to God during prayer. Because of this abstinence from physical sex they had few offspring and adopted refugees and orphans.

One such orphan was a boy named John who befriended Jesus. Jesus told John that he knew him before his birth. John had a sixth sense and could tell that Jesus was intimate with God above. The two were the smartest in their class, good friends, and the education that the Esseans provided would have a lasting impression on the two boys. When he grew up and became a leader in the Essean hierarchy, John the Baptis,t as he was later known, brought his followers over to Jesus

The Esseans had a variety of Jewish and foreign influences in their beliefs and customs. They were Jewish by race but spoke Greek. The Esseans were held in captivity in Persia and this is where they took on the Greek language and Persian customs. They believed in One God, observance of the Sabbath, and strict adherence to circumcision. The Esseans followed the Zoroastrian and Pythagorean sects. They also adopted ideas from Buddhism and Hellenism. Their beliefs about the sun, election of priests, and way of life are indications of their outside influence. To this day, there exists a secret order of Esseans that influenced the freemason's pursuit of a pure Christianity.

Most followers abstained from sex to help preserve peace and harmony in their lives. For this reason, they adopted children and took in converts. Some scholars speculate that the pent up desires caused by abstinence drove the Essean Priests to take advantage of these adopted children and that the practice carried on when they were later absorbed into the Christian Church. Young Jesus was being groomed as a convert. They wore white robes and carried a shovel to protect their excrement from the sun. They took secret oaths and were tested for years before becoming full members of the sect. They took vows to wear modest clothing. Like the Buddhists, they could not lie and did not tell outsiders about their rituals. The names of their angels and sacred books were guarded secrets. Herod did not make them take the oath of allegiance because their word was regarded by most people as sacred.

Jesus told them to avoid the city life and was pleased that they didn't take part in animal sacrifices. They were the first peace-loving communists, keeping their money in the collective and were not at all interested in war. They only used their swords for protection when traveling while Jesus always carried a knife with him. They shared each other's belongings as if they were their own.

One day while visiting the Esseans, Jesus needed to use the bathroom. He was told that this was not allowed on the Sabbath. So Jesus had to read and explain the scriptures with the wise older men who were assembled in order of age. On his way out, Jesus bumped into one of the older men. The old man shouted "unclean" and complained that he had to bathe to become pure again. The man said "I have been polluted by this dirty, homeless man and now I must wash again." Jesus found the constant cleaning to get in the way of his studies so he began to contemplate leaving the group.

The Esseans traded natural medicinal remedies with Jesus and showed him the healing power of minerals. They also traded magical secrets with Jesus and were amazed that all his predictions came true. This is why they respected him so much, for he agreed with their communist philosophy that ownership of homes should be in common with the group. Jesus noticed that even harvests and earned money went to the collective account, and he later used this system within his own militia.

One day the group was up before the sun rose as usual. They began to pray and summon the sun to rise. They said these prayers before eating. Jesus said he liked this idea but he found the silence during meals to be mysterious and unnecessary. He enjoyed talking at meal time because it was the only chance he had to converse with a group and these Esseans don't appreciate that. Jesus was cut off by an elder who said we only speak in turns during meals. During most meals they were each given modest portions, but at noon, they had a feast prepared by the priestly cast.

Jesus found that he could not convince them to drop their sexist biases. He told them that women could stay true to one man but they rejected this notion. Jesus reached into a hole in the sky and grabbed the gold codices of time and quoted from them but still he could not persuade his hosts to allow women to become leaders in their society. For this reason, Jesus decided to leave them and went on to Jordan.

Jesus said that Philo who taught him when he was a child in Egypt visited the Esseans also. Philo told Jesus and John that their actions will determine which ideas are adopted by future generations. He asked John to build the forces of discontent at home and told Jesus to go forth and learn about the world and come back when his talents are needed. So, the Christ child and Casper broke camp, and headed East across the great desert.

Crossing the desert was difficult and all the animals died of starvation except one camel that Jesus allowed to drink from his own water rations. Half of the entourage traveling with Jesus became sick from a rare disease which caused sores that were as sharp as thorns, and a rash that made them scratch until blood would pour from their flesh. Most would have died if Jesus had not performed a miracle and expelled the demon that was entering into the bodies of his companions causing them to have these symptoms.

A BOY IN BABYLON

The books of old tell us that this Child of God later wandered toward the East. He soon crossed the Tigris and Euphrates Rivers. This is where he acquired his military training with the Babylonians, a city with a great army. Here, Jesus learned the power of the sword, the power of authority, and the powers of terror, destruction, carnage, famine, killing, bloodshed, and death. He fought bravely as a mercenary. This is why later in life Christ commanded his disciples to carry swords. His disciple Simon cut off the ear of the servant of the high priest.

Christ then wandered through the desert for days in the brain-drying sun. He came upon a Bedouin tribe which was in the process of a harvest healing ritual. They saw that He was a man full of God's spirit and asked Him to join in on their celebration.

During the celebration Jesus allowed the Bedouins to see the face of God, and they became believers. Later he wandered to Persia, which is now Iran. Jesus had many episodes of anxiety and guilt, where he would see appendages cut from people around him, and limbless people screaming and running about in terror. Christ knew He was just reliving the death, gore, and mayhem that he had previously witnessed.

The child of God and Casper eventually traveled to Persia where the three wise men studied. People here studied many sciences including Astronomy and Chemistry. Here Jesus saw the great observatories that were dedicated to charting and studying the stars. Jesus learned how to perform more magic tricks here. Wise men in Babylon showed Jesus all the knowledge of Zoroaster and sent him to school.

In the early days of his stay in Babylon, Jesus was traded from school to school because of his great talents and constant travel. The masters of these religious schools were very strict. Often the rebellious Boy Jesus was called into the quarters of these clerics for punishment. Jesus Christ, like all of us, had to choose to externalize the pain and humiliation of punishment that comes from within. He learned to walk in pain, but as if one has truth or remorse on his side as if to vindicate his wrongs.

The boy Jesus lived a bright and disobedient boyhood. He constantly questioned authority and became engaged in the pursuit of truth and becoming the Teacher. He became Self-realized and God incarnate. He was known as the man sent down from Heaven to sacrifice for the many.

Jesus worked as a Prophet as well as a healer in Babylon and gave the people many great secret revelations. Jesus healed a woman who had not walked in twenty-seven years. Scribes recorded what he said and followed him on his future Journeys and some of these writings have survived.

Jesus believed only in one God and spread this idea to some Arabian sects. Some of these sects were very violent and Jesus was taught the art of war. He taught the desert warriors the advantage of using horses in battle. Jesus and the Arabians shared many secrets and trained each other's followers. Jesus told his disciples to explain the evil of idol worship. The all-knowing one said that in Six Hundred years a great and powerful prophet would be sent to remind people that God does not like images of his likeness. The benevolent one said, "the prophet God sends to this land will be a human as am I, and that we are all children of God."

In the time of Jesus, there were many female rulers in Persian lands, and he liked these people and they him. Since the land of Babylon was where agriculture began, male babies were considered valuable as field workers and were not killed at birth. Since there was an abundance of males, the females had many husbands. Jesus mated with these people, and they became the people of god along with the children he left in Jerusalem.

Jesus loved the Arabs, although in that time they were mostly worshippers of man made statues of gold that represented people transcended to godly status. During this era, many Arabs of the Tigris and Euphrates still made statues of gold and tried to love the object so much that it became a god. Jesus was violent toward these idolaters, but he knew that it wouldn't be for another six hundred years until his adjacent prophet came and brought the vengeance of Allah or God so that the souls of these lost people would be redeemed. These people wanted to worship Jesus as God, but Jesus said "I am your brother and I come to show you the Way to God."

Jesus was a Prophet who knew this issue would have to be learned and impressed upon people. He also said, "one day there will be such a dependence of people on objects and tools that they will lose sight of god, but eventually they will learn the heart of evil and not turn from it but endear it and claim that they invented these things on their own. Finally, these objects will be used against them and they will face god's wrath and turn back to him, but for many it will be too late."

He said, "A God who is seen by every nation from a different vantage point is a lost God. This is why war will come, but there will come a prophet six hundred years after me that will make every man know that god is one. He will also knock down the icons of idolaters and restore the fear of god into the people. Such a glory will require much death. So many men will die, that brother will have to marry his brother's widow, and men will take on more than one wife."

The greatest sermon Jesus delivered as a guest in Babylon was next to a marsh where there was food and a cool breeze for all to enjoy. His holy innocence said to those who had gathered that over time, weaker nations will destroy stronger nations. He compared the weaker nation to a leaf on the vine of the stronger. Unless such a Nation becomes independent, like a dandelion, it will wither and die. The dandelion kills the vine by usurping its resources and flowers.

Later, Jesus alluded to this future prophet and told the crowd that he would leave Babylon and Not Return. "This area will suffer for Six hundred Years and God then will send a great Profit and his word will bring salvation to a great part of the world. After this great prophet there will be a false son of God has that arrives on earth. There will be fifty years of war and starvation before I arrive to avenge his actions."

Jesus said, "in Two Thousand years a mighty force will come from the west to conquer Babylon's great leader. There will be much martyrdom and fighting against these forces. People will be close to translating the ancient Sumerian texts in museums in the land of Babylon. These texts are known to hold some of the greatest unrevealed secrets of God. On the third day this force of oppression will complete the true primary mission of destroying the museums which hold the secret texts of the ancients so that they cannot be translated, and the true will of god will not be known to the people for centuries. Then they will set about to steal the riches from this land and cart it home, as Alexander did Three hundred years before.

There will be weapons bloodier than a million knives. One leader will influence many with greater violence than has ever been seen in a religious struggle. He will be the false prophet and will be betrayed by his own followers and killed by the Western forces. The false prophet will destroy the new towers of Babel and look more like a reincarnation of me. Only the cries of the unborn can save you from what will come, and often the messenger will change the message. There will be a time when all who fight to change the world will be toiling for nothing. For the world will change on its own without the deeds of man, and God will see to it that his will is done." The elders did not want to alarm the people so they expelled Jesus from school for espousing such rhetoric.

In a street sermon Jesus said to the crowd, "I have talked to the dead. The fight will be over Jerusalem. It will be the righteous fighting my followers over the children of god. No one will speak of happiness and the word on all lips will be of war. The number that will perish in this century will be greater than all the plagues and all the famines.

God will part the skies, and all the seeds of evil will be allowed to descend upon the earth. Some of God's children will escape the wrath that will come to this planet. All the oceans will become stagnant and plants will not grow. So the seed that came from the heavens will be splashed on earth a second time. Some seeds will ascend into the heavens and out into the stars to spread what god has given us. I, Jesus, can explain these truths but only with time will you understand."

He said that "What is bad is good; there is no wrong; there is no evil in death. A Martyr attempts to achieve what he could not in life." This gave rise to the yin philosophy. He also said, "What is death but a fleeting moment when desires outlast habits? Perhaps death is a gift?" When he and his followers made it to an area that was the border between ancient Persia and ancient Arabia, they stopped and paused.

As day turned to night they set up camp and made plans to reach the mountains by the next day. As Jesus headed towards the mountains he again attracted large numbers of followers. Some would leave their homes and follow him for months. Many great followers came and went again. There were many disciples along the way, but only twelve at the end. Christ said there will be a great battle. The enemy will be elusive. At this time, Christ could have formed a guerilla army and brought it from the Middle East to Jerusalem, but chose not to. He knew the militia of God would need to be made of locals.

But Jesus taught: "Do not seek straight paths in darkness, possessed by fear. But gather force and support each other. He who supports his neighbor strengthens himself I tried to revive the laws of Moses in the hearts of the people. And I say unto you that you do not understand their true meaning because they do not teach revenge but forgiveness. But the meaning of these laws is distorted." Then a jealous teacher of worship sent his disguised servants that they should watch the people who listened and reported to him about his words to the people. But Jesus recognized the spies and slipped away once again into the night.

As he followed the old Alexandrian roads toward the hills of the Himalaya Mountains, he came upon the land of fire, where fire would burn from the ground. There were nomadic rulers and he was summoned to stay with a particularly powerful king and his family. The king's family ruled since Alexander the Great established their kingdom 300 years before Christ. The king was pleased with the ideas Jesus had of rebelling against Rome and keeping what was left of his wealth from Rome so that his people would not starve.

In Babylon and in India the boy Christ always had his pet Lion by his side. The other llamas and scribes in the east had companion tigers but only Jesus had a Lion. People would be amazed that he had a lion and Jesus would say I have nothing this animal is free. The benevolent one brought his lion with him all the way to India.

INSIGHT FROM INDIA

Later, Casper took the young prodigy to India after warning the parents of Jesus about the Omen of Fate. Casper told them that this omen, a strange beast that is now extinct, was the sign that God wanted Jesus to travel more and learn about the world. His travels to India were documented by the Brahman historians. Christ studied and proved to be a great teacher in the Orient. Jesus was known as the Buddha that showed them the way to gaining ultimate wisdom. It is said that for all time they will know him and love him as Saint Issa.

As a young teen, Jesus met Prince Ravenna. This prince was a traveler and very impressed with Jesus. Some say that Jesus met Ravenna in Jerusalem and asked his parents if he could study with him. When Joseph said no, the young Jesus sneaked out in the night and hid in the cargo of a caravan that was heading east. Other texts claim that Casper introduced Jesus to Prince Ravenna.

All sources agree that Jesus was able to study the wisdom of the Brahmins during his stay in India. Jesus was accepted as a student in the temple at Jagannath, and he learned the Vedas and scriptures of Buddhism. It was during this time that people started to call him Issa. Unlike other names given to people in this land Issa, has no original meaning and over the years has taken on the meaning of messiah. After some time, the common people here did not appreciate a Buddha from a far away land and called Jesus a leech of the land. For this reason, Jesus said farewell to Casper and Ravenna and traveled for a time on his own.

Documents say that a Jesus-like figure visited all of Asia around the time of his supposed death. For several years

Jesus preached to the island people from a raft of reeds. He taught the coastal Asians how to surf and fish.

It is said that he carried a heavy rock to the center of the largest island. Here, he met strange beasts and men that lived as animals. He told the aboriginals that this rock will be their hope and the Lord's truth will be known and shared throughout the world when this rock is turned upward. The glass sphere holding the stars rolls slowly yet conformingly consistently, smoothly and beautifully. The Journey of one thousand years begins with one small roll. These people were filled with hate and could not communicate his word and wandered aimlessly for centuries.

Jesus walked from the shores of the Indian Ocean up the Ganges river. He followed the trade routes toward the mountains. After a long journey with little food and water, he stumbled upon the holy city of Benares, located on the Ganges River. This is where he studied the Hindu art of healing, and was the student of the most successful Hindu healers. Jesus was at peace with him self during these years and learned to do mass healings. In the end he could make severed limbs re-grow. He also learned to take organs out of people's bodies and insert them into the bodies of others. He would stick needles into people and make all of their pains disappear.

There is a legend that Jesus built a great following along the Ganges River. One day he went before a crowd so large that some spectators had to stand in the river because the banks were too crowded. He explained to the starved people that the riches will go to the sons of the richest for a few more centuries and then God will even the score.

Jesus said, "The poor will rise up until the suffering of the indignant masses ends. There is no light on truth until I say these things. Only in this moment shall you feel the fear and wickedness of what is to lie before your every step. There is no justice until there is truth, and until the last of the wicked has walked through the rainbow in the heavens, and we all ask our selves if freedom is worth it. If the devil shall still knock at your door, you are to be assertive and tell him which way you walk, and that is the path of Christ."

The child of God then said, "If your children do not follow my word, Gargoyles will come up from Hell and lay feces, which will cause great plagues. Lepers will permeate society and limbs will fall from the bodies in great numbers. Appendages will appear on the streets in large numbers. Dead bodies will be scattered all over the roadways and little children in masses will be nibbling on torsos, while cries of the dying go unheard"

His group came upon a village of midget children with fangs that would ritualistically torture their animals during the day. The caravan was already worried as they listened to the screams of animals, and soon then they saw mutilated dogs that had more than one rope tying them to trees, eyes gouged out and limbs that had been chopped off.

The divine child began from his earliest years to speak of the one and indivisible God, exhorting the souls of those gone astray to repentance and the purification of the sins of which they were culpable. People came from all parts to hear him, and they marveled at the discourses proceeding from his childish mouth. Other child lamas were jealous and began to fight among themselves for the notoriety that Jesus had attained. Some even plotted to poison the one who brought light to the truth.

The adherents of the Vaishas and Shudras were struck with astonishment and asked what ritual they could perform that would cleanse their wrongs. Jesus bade them, "Worship not the idols. Do not consider yourself first. Do not humiliate your neighbor. Help the poor. Sustain the feeble. Do evil to no one. Do not covet that which you do not possess and which is possessed by others." Many, learning of such words, decided to kill Jesus. But the Christ Child was forewarned and left secretly by night.

Afterward, Jesus went into Nepal and into the mountains. Finding work designing a hidden city, he began to smoke Himalayan weeds that were all around him. The builders asked to see some miracles from this great god child. Jesus said that men should not try to see the eternal spirit with their own eyes, but should feel it in the heart and cleanse their soul. Jesus taught these people that it was wrong to give human or animal offerings because both were for the use of man. One day he fought to protect a baby goat that was to be offered to the gods in thanks for a male child. The servants said "but Master, you raise your fist to protect not only women but animals. Surely this is not the way of the future." But Jesus said "beware, of thy neighbor who divert men from the true path and who fill the people with superstitions and prejudices, who blind the vision of the seeing ones, and who preach subservience to material things."

A young boy had been caught shooting arrows at people traveling along the main road at night to scare them. Jesus said, "Do not put this boy to death for his evil is good. The fear he put in people's minds caused them to pray and worry about their family members. What has come from this evil is good. When a rich man gives money to the poor that is bad because then the poor people become spoiled and greedy. What is evil to some is good to others so judge not what is good."

A local villager in India said that Jesus preached beside a small pool under a great tree near the town bazaar, which now no longer exists. "Wherever power leads the meek, death and destruction are sure to follow." And many people had died and been executed in this town for following our lord. Some looked at Jesus and questioned his wisdom, but they fell down suddenly and died. The others who were present changed their minds and said he was god. Jesus lives in the hearts of Hindus and Buddhists. Then, he left the wise old Brahmans who returned after seeking the ultimate stage of existence in the forests.

The group accompanying Jesus went down to the river bank where women were cleaning their clothes in the river and men were gathering wood for a fire. Some in his group asked the lord why the locals do not just bury their dead. Jesus said, "Just as the ideas that I share with you will be reincarnated, so will our souls. There will be no pity for those who come back to life as a bird or a rodent, their screams will go unheard. These people worship a world that in transition, and we tend to want an afterlife that will be the same for all time." Then the lord decided to cure the Ganges river people of a million diseases. He asked the men to pile the sticks and burn the corpses before the tide carried them away. This is how the Hindu ritual of burning the dead was started and this method does keep diseases from spreading.

One day while picking wild mushrooms and smoking Salvia weeds in the forest, the Christ incarnate started to dwell in his melting flesh. Christ looked into a girl's face, and it would break into a million pieces. His head began to squeeze down as he felt his body enter the dimensions that are shut off from our existence. Here thousands of little people are eager to visit our minds and they spoke to Jesus telling him how they had been waiting for years to see him again. God entered the body of Jesus, and the Eternal Spirit, dwelling in a state of flux, awoke and detached itself for an indefinite period from the Eternal Being. In the guise of humanity, he could partake of the passions of the living. By separating his soul from its infinite state, the level of imperfection necessary to enter into this world, which is changeable and where misery abounds.

He realized after studying with some oracles that after death every being is reincarnated. Some choose their new manifestation of self, and some have memories of their past life. It is by man's works that God decides what form their next life will take. Some become fish, some bird, some serpent, but most turn into insects after their human life has ended. The final stage for a soul is to become a plant which meditates on a higher level than even the greatest sage on earth.

There are great legends of a handsome white man coming with many wives and spreading the word of peace to the world. These legends have been passed down by spoken word and still are popular among many tribes. They say for his blue eyes that any virgin would die for. There is the legend of the girl who stabbed herself twenty one times after being denied a walk with Jesus. There is the story of the water boy in Kashmir that would bring water to Jesus and his men in hopes of bedding with one of them. All of his followers had charisma, looks, long hair and this attracted throngs of people to every gathering and festival that they appeared at.

When Jesus left this area, the crowds cried for him to stay. Some accounts say his entourage had as many as fifty thousand young women offering their services to them. Many girls would offer to sew or do whatever those in Jesus' company wanted. There were many fights over who could carry his water. Sometimes, every young person from a village would follow him. Jesus noticed these peoples' infatuation with him and decided it was time to go. Some villages followed him as far as they could into the mountains and settled where they could travel no further.

ADOLESCENCE IN ASIA

Jesus continued north into the Himalayas and settled with followers of a great Buddha. For six years he applied himself to the study of the sacred sutras. Even with the humid Jungle heat and swarms of mosquitoes buzzing in his ears, Jesus would concentrate on his studies. He was sick of people paying homage to metals or stones. He felt man could be lifted into a higher form of self and that in the future man would be able to create new forms of life. For men are pawns in the games of those they try to please for no avail on into the centuries. Man will die off if he does not find a source of energy that will make it unnecessary to labor or work.

Jesus knew from what he learned from the sages in India that he would be reincarnated. In previous lives, he was a sun worshipper, author of the Book of the dead, architect of the Great Pyramid, Adam, Enoch and other great figures in ancient history. He knew he had a karmic debt or sin to work off because of the killing that he had already committed. The sages told Jesus that he would be reincarnate into an entity of the underworld after his death so that he could recruit some of the demons there to be informants working for the forces of Good. They told him that his dreams were true and he was the son of God and that his father in heaven wanted him to die so that all sins could be forgiven. Jesus went through seven initiations in his thirteenth reincarnation before finally becoming at one with The Christ.

As Jesus walked the picturesque passes of the Golan heights over the Punjab, he said I will incarnate during a holy war and walk these very passes, then down into the arid rocks of Kashmir into that inviolable secrecy of the Himalayas. Looking over the land of the Eternal Snows, Jesus and his guide looked for soldiers of god. The great Israelite Issa headed to Nepal and with his small band of warriors conquered many towns. Jesus rode a painted elephant and taught a small group of Mongols the power of the elephant in battle.

Returning to the wilderness of Hindustan, Jesus walked in the rain for days His caravan tiptoed across crevices in the rock that were often a three feet wide and a mile deep. "Our hearts stood still more than once during our perilous journey with Jesus", wrote one scribe. This scribe said that when he met Jesus, the Brahmans and sages considered him one of them already because he left his home to become one with god in the forests and could meditate for days at such a high level he could tell them what he said to them in their dreams and thoughts. They said he was the youngest sage ever because he had already had all the experiences of life and reached the highest level of thought. Sages would not ordinarily cut their hair, but Jesus kept his head shaved so that he did not stand out from the other young lamas. He didn't wear the white laced sandals that some of the other Adolescents wore but everyone respected and liked him.

The first Buddhist prophets established themselves in various countries of the world and Jesus was expected to bring their truths back to the people of his native land. Buddhist preaching was directed toward the tyranny they suffered under for centuries. One of The Christ Child's most trusted travel companions was a lama who wrote the great scrolls, describing the prophecies of Jesus that sat untouched in that frozen tent until Tibetan monks uncovered it 1800 years later. Then the monks hid the texts for two hundred more years before recently translating the story of the Prophet of Love visiting Tibet.

A TEENAGER IN TIBET

Jesus wandered up a caravan path all the way to Tibet where he read all the sacred manuscripts with the greatest sage of the Orient, a descendent of Meng-ste. Hearing of his unfamiliar accent, everyone came out to meet him and made sure the entire traveling group was well fed and had the greatest comforts available. The affable lama kept Jesus entertained throughout the following day with endless stories and knowledge.

On the day his caravan arrived, the doors of the temple opened wide, giving access to some persons disguised as animals, birds, devils, and monsters of every kind. Jesus soon realized that it was a religious ceremony. Young men, dressed as warriors, came out from the temple. They wore monstrous masks. Making an infernal din of screaming virgins, water pipes, and Swordfights, they gyrated around the ceremonial goddess, lifted high above. The prolonged spectacle was rewarded by an invitation from the chief lama for a drink of spirits in honor of the festival.

Ancient writings that were smuggled out of the residency of the Dali Lama tell what Jesus did there. After learning how to worship peace and tranquility, Jesus would start spouting long prophecies that haunted him about the future, saying there is no love, just hatred. "God tells us that heads will be smashed and limbs will be torn from bodies. Poisonous gasses will be pumped into sealed off houses. With multitudes dying, they will fly a Black flag that symbolizes a rejection of authority." (TIB 3:32) Christ felt that if everyone was being followed as he was, then they all would be a little paranoid and feel like the messiah.

The monks knew that Jesus had a direct link to the ultimate stages of reality and that he could communicate with the oneness of existence. The sages sprinkled Jesus with the spores of mushrooms and hallucinogenic roots and herbs and the bark of trees. And Jesus partook of these and saw many visions of God. Later, Jesus returned to these wise men or great Buddha's and Sages.

Jesus was joyously accepted and loved by people of the lower class. Jesus preached in the temples, the markets, and wherever people gathered. One day, a woman brought her dead son to Jesus where people had gathered around. Jesus laid his hand on the boy's head, and the child sprang up healed. Jesus performed many such healings while in Tibet.

The followers of the Tibetan loved Jesus and when the time of his departure came they felt sorrow. As a result of his leaving, children wept and mothers committed suicide, because much guilt followed. They felt as if he had left because they did not show enough love while he was there. They felt guilty because they did not show how much they were influenced by his words and examples. The ones who survived the mass suicides, joined hands and espoused their love for one another. A messenger was sent to Jesus to tell him that they loved his message and that it changed their lives. The sad thing is that this messenger never made it to Jesus, because he was killed by a neighboring tribe that was jealous that Jesus had not visited them as well. Researchers trying to uncover what Jesus did after this sad departure often have to rely on stories passed down and local legends.

The Legends of Jesus go all the way to Mongolia where he rode on an elephant caravan from India. It is said that he prophesized the rise of a leader that would take elephants over the Alps and conquer the world. Many people don't want to believe that Jesus helped shape Hinduism, Buddhism, and

Islam in ways that have been suppressed by leaders of each religion. The monks of these eastern religions also consulted with and influenced Jesus.

A monk came to Jesus and told him the secrets of the universe. He said to Jesus, "long ago there was a great amount of industry and as many lights on earth as in the heavens, but a great fireball turned off all the lights. The people should never become dependent on their own makings again, for if they do, they will toil forever. It is up to you, Jesus, to set the captives free. You alone must make sure that the symbol of god is one. For this plan is in the best interest of all of us." Then Jesus thanked the monk for his advice and said farewell to the people of this land.

Sources are not clear on how Jesus made it out of Tibet and how long it took him. This part of the story may be a mystery lost to antiquity. We do know that he went to Rome before going home.

NEGOTIATIONS FAILED

The last time Jesus met with Melcher they talked for a long time about how to deal with the invaders from the west. Melcher told Jesus to first try imparting logical knowledge to the Romans. Jesus liked this idea of explaining how the people of the Middle Eastern Nations could live in harmony if the Westerners could act as trading partners rather than occupiers. So before heading home, Jesus went to Rome to talk to the leaders and convince them that they should pull their armies out of the Middle Eastern nations.

When he first reached Rome, he was a young man and enjoyed himself. He was treated as an ambassador from the east because he could speak any language. He saw many plays being performed and was introduced to the latest military technology the Romans had. He was impressed with the bath houses and the free love that went on in Rome. He read Roman philosophy and couldn't help but take time to study their culture and ideas.

After awhile, he started to press his mission of encouraging and convincing the Western leaders to pull their armies out of Israel. He found that the more he tried to persuade them about how logical it was to pull out of Isreal and appease the people, the more resistance he came across. Some challenged him to debates in the public square, but the audiences were already convinced that he came to weaken the Romans strong hold on Israel and so he faced mockery and scorn. He increasingly found himself arguing against ignorant Roman patriots who saw any movement of their armies out of a land as a loss of world domination and influence, and ultimately as a threat to their own well being.

Jesus tried to explain to the Romans that any nation would fight an invading army and that the resistance to outside rulers was natural. He said, "Would you not fight as your fore fathers fought when outside armies tried to invade your country?" At first many in the court of Cesar agreed with him, but later, they sent him to lower level leaders because they did not want to hear such logic.

There were many reasons the common Romans rejected his pleas. They said it would cause them to pay more for goods that came from the Middle East because trade and commerce would not flow as freely. Many said that it was better to fight the Monotheists there now; otherwise, they would have to fight them in Rome in the future. In the end, Christ found that Roman leaders unleashed him onto the ignorant masses who were intolerant of the idea of Peace.

This made Jesus feel withdrawn and he began to wander and panhandle in Rome. He found that beggars are some of the most interesting people he had met. After seeing what it was like to be a beggar, Jesus met Philosophers. He indulged in cravings for hemp and wine while engaging in deep conversation.

He walked to other parts of the Roman Empire. There are indications that he made it all the way to the British Isles. He told the people of modern day Ireland that the way to tell how long ago a race was seeded on earth is by the separation distance of their eyes, and not their skin color. Ancient Hermetic writings found in England also indicate that he considered discrimination between races a sin because it makes a mockery of Creation.

After traveling around the Roman Empire, he decided negotiating with the Romans was futile because all they knew was power. Jesus looked into Gods eyes, reached in and pulled out the Spirit. This dynamic trinity, Super-God, the Over-man, the ultimate stage of reality, will save us from the dark forces of the universe. Christ felt that he should start to consolidate his own band of followers, maybe even a new sect.

He had many followers wherever he went so he knew he needed to find a way to link all his followers. He met many people here, and it is said that when he left, he sent a group of ten followers north to spread his own word and fifty followers to stay and keep sanctuary for his revolutionaries. He then headed home by boat.

The night before he left, God visited him in a dream and told Jesus that he could no longer perform miracles unless it was to convert people. God did this so that Jesus could experience the pain and sadness that goes along with humanity. So, he was already worried about going by boat when they ran into a horrible storm. The waves were ten feet tall and as wide as a boat. Many went overboard and were not saved. The boat limped to shore in what is now Lebanon. Some asked Jesus why he let these people drown, and he explained how his miracle powers had been restricted and everyone said they still had faith in Jesus.

The group he was with decided to go through the forest and walk south to Israel. He knew there would be no happy ending in walking through the forest because bandits and wild animals were a constant threat there. They took the hash trader trails and staggered into the wilderness. In the forest there were some settlements, but they were far and few between. At the last watering hole, they divided what rations remained and prayed for God's mercy. Soon they found themselves walking for days and not seeing other people. Jesus was at peace here and found it the most tranquil part of all his journeys. This was the great wilderness and Jesus loved the tall pine trees and the way the forest creatures had a symbiotic chant and greeting.

OUT OF THE WILDERNESS

As soon as the Christ walked out of the wilderness, multitudes started to follow him. In fact, many were very close to Jesus and began to write and talk of him before any of the disciples, including Magdalene, even met him. Jesus was carrying a rose and of those who did not survive the journey, he said, "Those who died along the way should be grateful that they died and were eaten, for those who follow me further will die an even more cruel death than starvation."

As he was walking, he noticed how meaningless the lives of those he saw were. Christ began to wonder if there was any purpose to his own life. "Have I wandered about passing out the secrets of god in search of more truth in vain? Will anyone ever even know that I existed? Is my importance in this world no more than that of a faint star in the heavens?"

This doubt continued to trouble him, but at the same time, he realized how insignificant we are and how the death of a son brings a family's love to the surface. He remembered spreading the word in India that there is no wrong, for bad brings about as much good. If there is no wrong, there should be no hate. He realized at this point that to forgive thy enemy is easy, because the wrong he does is out of jealousy born of ignorance that his own life is meaningless. "The only thing to hate is hate itself," he would say.

On this day he relayed some other things that he had learned during his travels. Christ said, "There are two opposing forces in this world. There is the force of individual freedom which brings about a desire for good in an individual's life. Then there is the force of equality where a group of people unite and try to distribute wealth for the good of the society. Neither one is necessarily evil or corrupt, but the fight will plague man for centuries. One of my missions here on earth is to explain this dichotomy to the common man. My word will be misrepresented so that the power of the secret brotherhoods is preserved until a New Faith arises from the ashes of the old." The people with him were not quite ready to grasp the importance of what he was saying, but were glad to hear his lesson.

After teaching these things to his followers, they came upon a girl that had her arm smashed in a rock quarry. Her father was an idolater so when Jesus replaced the arm with a new one, the new one had one extra finger. Some are more trivial. For example, he produced from wine a new drink that brought sudden hallucinations. He produced substances that when smoked "made one perspire as if in the depths of hell on earth and vomit all his insides and still want to smoke more. He also developed other substances that made people relax." Before heading home, Jesus and some early followers passed through a village where some of his sermons were found hidden under a church centuries later.

There was also some turmoil because many who had followed him from Asia were discriminated against by his newer followers despite Jesus speaking against it. Many who had traveled with him also did not want to be ruled by or have to fight against the powerful Roman legions. Also, Jesus himself told a crowd that Angels had called many of them home to become wise men in their own lands. He had already started gathering his early band of Biblical Apostles. One of the first towns they came to was Magdala, and this is where he reunited with his soul-mate that he had not seen in years.

THE WEDDING

A baby boy came to Jesus and impressed him with knowledge of rituals and practical knowledge. When the boy turned five years old, he died. He rotted for ten days before Jesus arrived at his family's tomb. The boy was one of the sons of a great Arab Emir that held the Princes of Magdala hostage. Jesus brought the boy back to life and traded him for the Princess's freedom. Jesus told the Emir his son would age fast and that for all future generations, his sons offspring might bear children that age fast. A miracle ransomed for the freedom of a captive will be a tainted blessing. There are other so called half miracles that Jesus performed that are omitted from the bible. He then brought the Princess to her home which is the kingdom known as Magdala in Syria.

The Princess came up and kissed Jesus and he was very pleased. This was the girl he called Mary that he met long ago in Africa. He knew not to tell even his most trusted companions that she was a Grand Daughter of Cleopatra the Great. Jesus whispered to her, "How are the children?" She assured him that they were fine and that Sarah their daughter was showing much promise in her studies. There was no need for Jesus to mention his past with Mary because it was assumed that Jesus being the semen of God knew everyone before they were born. Also, the fact that she was a descendant of Cleopatra the Great would bring only criticism from any Jew living in that era.

Most of the disciples were pleased that Jesus found joy in the company of this princess. They nicknamed her Magdalene after the city from which she came, and since Jesus called her Mary, she became known as Mary Magdalene from then on. Some disciples were naturally jealous of Mary because everyone always fought for the attention of the lord.

However, some of the disciples made a vow to protect her forever because they were devoted to anything that Jesus held dear.

The king of Magdala was impressed with all Jesus had accomplished, and asked Jesus to marry his adopted daughter, the Princess of Magdala. "Take care of her in your far away land and remember that she is a free spirited princess who deserves dignity and respect." Jesus told him that he respected all women over men, and that she would be treated as if she were a goddess. The people around started to worship Magdalene. We will make her "the sacred feminine" they said. Jesus warned Magdalene, though, that the worship of her would be forced underground as they headed east towards Jerusalem. We must protect our daughter and I will show you which of my disciples to trust in this matter.

There were almost no unmarried rabbis outside of the small Essean sect during the time of Jesus, so it was natural that he should take a bride. The Ceremony of Marriage was where Jesus disagreed with John and his Essean ideology. Because John started the church in Rome, the Essean's later became leaders of the revolution that Jesus started. After being influenced by Jesus, the Esseans decreed that only the clergy must refrain from having sex, but sexist sentiments and taboos toward sex became a growing cancer in the later church.

All of the arrangements were in order for the wedding, but the wine Jesus brought had run out. Magdalene worried that the wedding would become a disaster because so many guests were coming and there was no more wine. So, Jesus turned six jars of that morning's rain water into a river of wine for the guests.

All types of common people were invited. This included thieves, social outcasts, prostitutes, common sinners and the like. The wedding was at Cana a city in the kingdom. Jesus said the wedding feast that he has prepared is like the Kingdom of God. There will be more food in heaven than is needed to feed one thousand tribes. The taste of the food will be like no other, and each person will become so full that food will come out of their mouths. Wine will flow like water in the kingdom.

Jesus was eager to show his followers that marriage is acceptable. But he told all that were present to keep this wedding secret because the westerners named him an enemy combatant for declaring that Rome would fall. The king gave Jesus Magdalene, his most prized daughter. John performed the ceremony and all present were in a festive mood until some jealous feelings that his friends were feeling started surfacing in the drunken conversations.

A conflict arose when Mathew asked Jesus why he kissed Mary in a different way than he kissed them. Christ kissed her often on the mouth and this caused some disciples to ask why he would act as if he loved her more than them. Jesus replied that he loves all men and women equally. The way Magdalene held sway over the emotions and actions of Jesus sometimes offended the other disciples, but they kept their jealous thoughts to themselves while Jesus was alive. Mary Magdalene said, "Jesus, your friends seem to get jealous of our love and how often you hold and kiss me." Jesus said, "I told Peter and my men that you are to be revered as a queen and a princess and they may have misunderstood my devotions." Jesus went and talked to Mathew and some others and by the end of the day they were all holding hands in a show of friendship and the conflict ended for the time being.

Many said that Jesus and Mary made a beautiful bride and groom. Jesus had grown very tall of stature for a man of his time in any land. He had beautiful deep eyes that would appear blue one day, and then brown the next. It was said that all women looked twice at him. Magdalene was a beautiful bride. Mary had thick long hair and the pair looked as if they were made for each other.

When the wedding celebration was drawing to a close and guests were saying goodbye to the bride and groom, someone sounded the alarm that soldiers were near and warriors were needed to ambush them. A group of fighters gathered, but they found out that there were too many soldiers to confront. So all the men had to leave briskly and stay the night in the cold mountains and this was their honeymoon. This is where they met the man whom the disciples called the black magician. He showed them all the pagan rituals and they practiced judgment of the dead. This is how Jesus and Mary spent their honeymoon, cold and damp, practicing magic while hiding from Roman soldiers.

By the next morning the soldiers had passed and it was safe to move about and make breakfast. Jesus said farewell to his disciples of the east that stayed with him to witness the wedding. Then Jesus and those that remained started on the journey to his homeland, the birthplace of David. He had been warned that he would run into insurgents on the way, and that they would ask his group to join their struggle against the Roman occupation.

A BLOODY REVOLUTION

Many in Jesus' clan joined the insurgency. Jesus decided to fight the Romans as well. He didn't ever see a point to wars; he just wanted to partake of the human experience when he fought before. He carried a sword and ordered his followers to carry swords. Even the Bible says that the disciples carried swords when it mentions that Jesus ordered his disciple to cut off the ear of a guard of the high priest who came to get Jesus when he was betrayed. The people who didn't fight made shields and supported the insurgency in other ways. The charismatic Lamb of God became a great leader. Gasper was a great inspiration for the insurgency and raised funds for weapons. In the end this revolution gave Jesus the ideas that allowed him to start converting the entire world over to a monotheistic religion.

Jesus was a great warrior who won many battles for the insurgency. He taught many how to use lantern oil as a weapon. They would pour the oil onto the road making puddles. As soon as a roman chariots drove by, they would ignite the oil and the flash fire would burn the soldiers to death. The insurgents following Jesus killed many soldiers using this improvised, burning device. Thousands of heathen soldiers were killed from these tactics and the people of the western world became weary of the war. Jesus said that this is the fate of the non-believer, god-willing. The mortal act of killing still fascinated Jesus but he began to see the wrong in the emotion of power that slaughter brought on.

After one great battle, his followers had to hide out deep in the desert and most of the horses died of starvation. Jesus was very upset that his horse died because they were given to him as a gift from Gasper, who was helping deliver supplies to the insurgents.

Jesus and his group had to stay hidden in caves for weeks at a time. Sometimes, there was no food or water. Here they invented all sorts of weapons. They made trip wires that were connected to cauldrons of hot boiling oil that spilled all over the soldiers. The called themselves the messiah militia, the First Army of God, or the Messiahs Martyrs Brigade. Jesus was constantly recruiting new followers and spreading his message at gatherings. A few of the women were armed and would fight in the battles; most chose to cook or tend to wounds.

Jesus rode a white horse during the early part of his militancy and became known as the holy knight. Jesus said, "We will slaughter our enemies like a lamb ready for sacrifice!" We must smite our enemies by the sword, was a constant battle cry. Jesus was considered the greatest military leader to come about in three hundred years. Many were aware that he was related to Alexander the Great. In one account, he took on ten thousand Romans with only a few hundred men and many soldiers were slain, and blood gushed over the desert ground and dried up, leaving a red road for his men to travel on. The entrails of slain soldiers were left to feed the vultures. Jesus stomping on skulls marveled at the body parts that littered the desert as limbless torsos screamed up to him asking him to end their misery. This victory was considered one of his greatest contested miracles.

There was much blood spilled. He wanted to feel as much as he could the emotion of taking mortal lives. He smashed heads together and left pools of blood on the ground. He said there was no death for the righteous. He said, "War is the same as killing a man on the street. War is the same feeling as taking someone from people for no reason. If people truly believe in one god then there would be no sectarian violence. The bones of the wicked will be ground to dust and baked into bread to feed the righteous and bring purity. On the battlefield love is being stomped out one life at a time. Every day the same love is being killed."

There were many battles and much blood was spilled by his followers. Many were disturbed by the blood that just formed red mud in the sand. He wondered why man needed to fight in this way. On the way home from one battle, the disciples said they had to walk past the haunting ghosts of those who had been slaughtered.

Barnabas said to Jesus that when I sold my land and gave the money to your followers I thought it would be used to buy fine linens for you, but it was used to buy weapons for the resistance as you promised. Barnabas had lost a lot of men fighting a guerilla war against the Westerners occupation of Israel. He is not considered one of the twelve apostles, but he followed Jesus and protected his men many times. He said to Jesus, "My hands tremble with guilt what is good and honor, would there be good without evil? How many must die?" Jesus replied that many would die in the war against Tyranny. He also said that in the future, there would be greater military leaders fighting for righteousness than the world had ever seen. Jesus also told him that after the Romans fell, other governments would be toppled before God could set up a truly free society that is free of coercion.

A zealous nationalist who wanted to drive the Romans out of the cities, claimed to be the savior until he joined forces with Jesus. His name was Simon and he pledged allegiance to Jesus. Simon's pirate army used tactics that often resulted in bloody conflict. They would pose as fishermen and raid trade ships and plunder their gold.

One day there was a pause in the fighting and Jesus told his men to go to the taverns in the town and he would buy them all a new invention called beer. While sitting at the bar with some warriors, Jesus warned his followers to be weary of nations that change allegiances quickly and of multitudes following a false ideology. There will be those who want to fool the old into believing that their generation was noble when, in fact, it was cruel and uncaring and led to many problems that arise later.

A one-eyed midget came up to Jesus and said "Master, shall we slaughter the infidels who worship the sun?" The lord said that one day this worship will have some validity because the sun has crystals which send off signals to all the creatures on the earth. It is picked up by the snake coils inside us and this is how a bird knows to behave like a bird and a man knows how to behave as a man. As we age, the coils do not work as well and people rely on the old signals and become stuck in their ways. This is how signals from heaven are sent to us by our souls that reside with God. This is why we should not slaughter any people because all are different and all have a place in Gods plan he said.

Although their were many successes using guerilla hit and run tactics, his militia was no match for Roman legions on a battlefield. After one particularly bloody battle, the young Christ had lost many of his best fighters and apologized for leading his people into the trap set by the western invaders and their allies. There were bodies scattered all over an apple orchard and the surrounding hillsides, and blood was flowing so thick that a small lake of blood was formed. Jesus began to realize that it would be better to use centuries of ideological warfare, rather than continue loosing so many men.
Jesus walked away feeling betrayed by some of the militia leaders and frustrated about his own decisions. He was in low spirits and walked further into the hills with the wounded and survivors to contemplate his next move.

For a time his men started employing suicide missions where two would go in with a vat of oil and burnout an entire tent holding westerners. They were so determined that giving their life for Jesus was no problem. Hundreds started signing up to join their group. In one mission they use a hundred men and ran into a base of Romans with vats of oil. They were able to burn many soldiers, but Jesus lost some of his most trusted militia leaders in the mission. This loss of good, loyal men started to wear on him.

After all the fighting and trauma, Jesus walked away trembling. Christ became a shell of his old self; he was dejected depressed, and angry. Jesus was sad about loosing so many in suicide missions. He went up to the Golan hills to gather his thoughts.

In the hills meditating, Christ thought about what a waste is was of these good men whom he loved so much. He thought about ways that he could show the world the devotion that his men had to God at the instant they die. Then all of a sudden, what the Book of Dead said about the power of death made total sense. What if he could win over the hearts of ordinary westerners, until they didn't support the Armies coming to the Middle Eastern Nations? He began to wonder. Each one could go to a different city and wake the world up to his cause and at the same time spread the oneness of God. He decided to send his followers to preach in his name and have them die the way he planed to die at the hands of those filled with hatred ignorance and fear. Since each one has already volunteered for a suicide mission, he could direct them to different nations to spread his word until they were martyred.

INSURGENCY ENDED

When he was finished mourning his losses, he returned from the heights and started his ministry. Many were disheartened that Jesus decided to put down his arms and allow his militia to scatter. Even though God never let Jesus use miracles in military pursuits, his people were much more successful than their enemies. Jesus knew that the people were tired of war as well as having their relatives vanish in the night, never to be seen again. So, he left behind scattered pockets of zealots that went their own ways, some continuing to fight and others giving up the struggle.

Jesus decided to start a passive resistance. He taught the people about nonviolent resistance and how to boycott and not cooperate with the Roman invaders until they had no choice but to leave. Jesus said, "After we drive out the non-believer invaders, we will build a new society from the ashes. We will build a society that has no need for government and everyone will live in harmony according to God's word. If only I had a thousand lives to give to the cause of injustice and the annihilation of invaders." He remembered what God wanted and that it was his choice how to achieve God's will. This is when he finally decided to convert the Romans to a Judeo-Hindu monotheistic belief system rather than fight them militarily. The peace loving Esseans were pleased with his decision and offered any assistance to his ministry while the Pharisees still saw him as a threat to their authority and helped in his eventual capture.

"Your sins will kill me, I will have to die for you", he told his companions. "How many times must I die for you? Will you be glad when I am dead? The world is wrong. The leader of the western world is out to get us. Most sects are out to get us; the nationalists, the Atheists are all out to kill us.

Only the paranoid will have hope in a world gone wrong. My true word will be hidden for two thousand years, and guilt will be the tool of tyrants. Fear not because we will prevail in the end because man cannot kill my spirit."

The Christ-child said, "I must die, as the ultimate sacrifice because man sinned. Many will go into the everlasting punishment, but the righteous elite into eternal life." By not fighting mercenaries sent from the west, Jesus would influence their minds.

This is the fundamental shift in the way Jesus decided to conquer the world for God and to do his part in fulfilling the prophecies of the Old Testament scriptures. So Jesus laid down most of his arms and started a ministry that would one day convert the Roman Empire to his teachings. He told his men to stop performing suicide missions with fire. He told his followers that instead of being martyrs in battle as they had been doing, they will all become martyrs of peace, dying for faith instead of killing a few Romans in fires. The messiah said "No longer will we be Lucifer's love children; we will stand for the end of wars on earth so that the poor may survive."

MARTYRDOM FOR PEACE

The Lamb of God realized that he should convert the Westerners by peaceful means rather than beat them at their own game, war and deceit. He knew the Old Testament scriptures well, and now he saw his place in their fulfillment. Because he was the son of God, only his martyrdom would redeem the sins of mankind. Jesus remembered what Balthasar and the Babylonians had told him about not being so rigid that he would break and he thought that this was the mistake he had made. He had so many followers willing to Martyr themselves for his cause why not send them as teachers of his word to all the far off lands to convert people. Let the intolerant ones crucify them and let them be willing to die for his cause. In so doing they would show people that their faith was stronger than the sword. And so from this day on he prepared his followers to be killed by the infidels as a sacrifice to show the strength of their faith, thereby converting some whose sins could be forgiven.

A secret gathering of his core followers was organized to prepare them not only for his martyrdom, but for the sacrifices that they would make for the cause as well. Jesus enjoyed these gatherings organized by Joanna, Mary, and Magdalene because they all felt it stimulated conversation of their core principles and beliefs. It is these three women who convinced him that with his charisma, he could start a movement that would convert the world. There are over one hundred women who followed him from the beginning of his ministry and helped organize meetings or the travel group or traveled with them for some amount of time.

There are 12 Apostles to represent the 12 tribes of Israel, but Jesus had many more apostles. There were other apostles that Jesus chose to represent tribes of other nations.

He had at least seven female apostles chosen to represent women's causes. He asked Joanna to represent women in the east after he died. Jesus knew how each of the twelve apostles would die and he told each of them how their Martyrdom would occur. Although not all the Apostles were able to attend this meeting or even had received word of it in time, he allowed all a chance to speak and some of what was said was recorded by a scribe and has recently been translated.

Jesus said that he will have Judas act as if he had betrayed him. Jesus knew he would be sentenced to die on a cross and would live on and go to places that no one has returned from. He said, "Judas is willing to kill himself in the first peaceful suicide mission ever for the insurgency, for he will kill only himself, and no Romans. He will hang himself over the valley outside Jerusalem and his body will smash into pieces. Then I will rejoin you my brothers and we will be happy. Finally, all of us will scatter to far away lands and train others to resist the governments. Then I want all 70 apostles to spread my word across the land as a disease would spread throughout entire populations. After one hundred, years there will be ten thousand apostles and the number will grow as the number of insects grows in a nest."

Most people believe Jesus actually died and was reincarnated. Some historians say that he knew of plants that would make him seem dead for days, so that his body could be carried to a tomb. There are some references in Coptic bibles to a twin of Jesus that was crucified in his place. This is where faith comes in, but the message is still the same.

Christ predicted that Thomas would be martyred in India with a spear through his heart for preaching the word of Christ to heathens. Jesus told him, "Blood will spew forth and you will smile and say praise Issa the Christ." Jesus told Thomas go to India with most of the disciples for immediate safety and spread his word around the world. According to tradition, Thomas traveled to Persia and South India, where he founded the ancient Mar Thomas Church. It is said that Jesus showed him how to sing his prayers, and this is one of the things he brought to the world.

The three wise men also went to India after the death of Jesus and continued to spread the glory of his life. Thomas the Apostle baptized the three and made them each Bishops. As Jesus predicted these three wise men each lived to be one hundred years old and after meeting for a final Christmas died within days of each other. Even revenue from their relics, helped raise money for building a system of churches that would act as fortresses to protect the offspring of Jesus. The remains now lay beneath a Gothic Cathedral in Germany providing a monument reminding people of the glory of the life of Jesus.

Andrew would be martyred in India as well. "You will add to the Upanishads and other sacred texts while you translate them", Christ told him. Andrew was tortured and martyred in India. As he was being whipped, a scribe quotes him as saying "Relinquish Control of your life over the Christ. Accept him into the very essence of your Being."

Christ said that future generations would honor the names of disciples after they are martyred. He told them that your names will be used for the unborn on earth for eternity and their will be many gifts for you in heaven as well." As Jesus predicted, Peter asked to be crucified upside down because he did not feel that he was worthy to die as Christ did.

The chosen one told Bartholomew to start a hidden Coptic church in Egypt and Martyr himself in India. The lord already knew Bartholomew Nathaniel when they met. Bartholomew went to India and translated Mathew's text as

Jesus told him to.   Historical accounts say that Bartholomew was beaten, crucified, and beheaded in Armenia as Jesus prophesized.

James would be thrown of a temple by scribes of the Pharisees who thought that he had misrepresented them. Then the entire town stoned him and the brains were clubbed out of his head exactly the way Jesus predicted.

Jesus told Mathew to go to Egypt and Ethiopia and spread the word of God and Martyr yourself for our cause. The son of God said, "They will stab you for spreading my word to a godless people and you will smile with blood coming out of your mouth and tell them that Christ will forgive them."

Paul was instructed to establish a church in Syria and to have Barnabas lead it. The Lord told him to go on various missionary journeys to bring the Gospel to the Gentiles. He was told that he would be imprisoned twice and then martyred after preaching the Lord's word. In Rome, Paul had his head chopped off for fulfilling the lord's wishes.

The other apostles were also eventually martyred for spreading the ideas of feminism, tolerance, and salvation through Christ. Andrew was crucified in Greece for telling the stories of his time with Jesus. Philip was arrested in Carthage for converting powerful women and given a death sentence. Bartholomew was killed in India. In Persia, Simon was killed for saying that if the sun God was the one true God, then it had a son named Jesus. Matthias was burned in a huge fire in Syria. John lived to an old age taking care of the mother of Jesus, but some records indicate that he may have been poisoned after her death.

Banished to a lonely island, John received visions of the future and words from the Lord of seven churches. Later, John survived being thrown into boiling oil and was banished to a desolate island. These visions and some of his surviving letters formed the Book of Revelation. Jesus said, "After I leave, I want you to take care of my mother as if she is your own."

Over time, James became the leader of the church and held much sway as Jesus predicted. James stayed in Jerusalem where the church money was. The gospels give no indication as to how powerful James became. James was later stoned to death by the Fundamentalist Jews in Syria.

As for Peter, he decided it would be safer to go to Rome and work on building the church there. It is believed that he was killed there for proclaiming his love for Jesus. Some records indicate that the secret brotherhood tortured him in an attempt to gather information about were Mary was hidden. The meeting began to end Just as Jesus was describing the fate of Peter.

As this secret meeting came to a close and idle talk began to consume the crowd, some foreign men approached the gathering. They were Roman mercenaries on their way home and spoke of getting revenge for some lost comrades unless they were given gold. Peter, sensing danger, drew his sword and asked the men what their business was. Jesus took out a torch and splashed lamp oil in their faces and the men ran. As they left, the men threatened to return and burn all of the disciples. They said that one day they would kill Jesus and all of his followers and chase the children of Jesus and their children until the prodigy of Jesus terminated. Jesus was not afraid and led his men along the Sea of Galilee which flows into the Dead Sea.

DEAD SEA GATHERING

The following Spring brought calm skies, and it was on such a pleasant day John the Baptist gathered a group of about four thousand Essean followers on the shore of the Dead Sea where it meets the sea of Galilee. They were acting as gracious hosts to the disciples who had been staying with them for several weeks celebrating the new peace that Jesus brought. Jesus presented John with his newest invention, a table and chairs, where people can dine together and sit upright. John presented a chalice from the age of their childhood to sit on the table. John said let this Cup represent the unity of God and that the circle comes back in on itself but is open to the world of liquid and the word of air. The Esseans were pleased that Jesus was still fixated on the message that God is one that he learned was handed down by Moses in Essean Schools.

The Esseans were more withdrawn than other sects. They preferred being in the wilderness far from the ruthless Roman rulers. It was understood that the Esseans and the Pharisees negotiated an end to the insurgency, but these groups also undermined the ministry of Jesus Christ long before the formation of the early Church.

John the Baptist studied with Jesus as a child and now he was a great Essean leader. Esseans knew the time had come for the messiah to enter the world and considered John their messiah. One day John was dunking heads cleansing them. John looked up on the bank of the river and said to Jesus, "I have been waiting for you messiah". Jesus asked John to baptize him. John said he cannot baptize a Rabbi that was greater than himself, but Jesus insisted. The Lamb of God wanted to show that he was in solidarity with sinners. Then John told his followers to obey Jesus and proclaimed him to be the new leader of the Melchizedek priesthood. After this, throngs would follow Jesus from every sect. The poor grew to love Jesus. No longer was he the novice boy who left the Essean schools over a decade earlier.

Rabbi Jesus and his hosts agreed that knowledge is the best path to God, and that material possessions are a distraction. They told Jesus that they longed for death as an escape from the prison sentence that living in their physical bodies imposed on their souls. They taught Jesus that the soul would live forever and would ascend into heaven once delivered from the bondage of life. They had a mystical bent that appealed to Jesus. Like the Greeks they taught that there is only happiness in heaven, and this is where the good people will end up. The bad people will be tormented for eternity in the depths of Hell and damnation, and their souls cast out to wither in the light of the sun. Jesus said," for me the body will be resurrected along with my soul." Jesus knew the Essen's were staying closer to God by avoiding reliance on material possessions.

One day, Magdalene wanted a new pair of sandals, but Jesus told her that she must wear out the old pair. She did not like this, so she scraped hers along rocks until they were worn. The Essen's did not like this and told Jesus. Jesus said that her rich upbringing made her a materialist, but that he was bringing her back to God. Jesus wanted to show in addition to avoiding the material world and helping others, the Essen's needed more for complete salvation.

Jesus then tried to show the Essean's the true path to redemption. We care for the sick and take in strangers so we will be guaranteed a place in heaven", said one of the Essen's. Jesus told him that this is good that you take in strangers and consider all men equal and respect justice and truth, but that will not alone guarantee you a place in heaven.

One man came to Jesus; he was starving because he had been excommunicated from the group for using the services of a slave girl. He said to Jesus," I cannot eat food prepared by outsiders and the others will not feed me so should I die here of starvation. Jesus had an idea and said that if we allow forgiveness of sins then fewer of us will starve to death. Rabbi Jesus explained that one reason it was not good to have servants is because they bring immoral influences into a house.

Another member of this sect told Jesus their rules prohibited him from uttering a lie and so when a woman asked if she was attractive he had to tell her no. The man claimed that for this a court of one hundred elders found him guilty of insulting the woman and punished him. Jesus urged some of the leaders of this sect to always use a common sense approach when interpreting rules and laws that are in scripture.

The Essen's elected leaders and they had a system where all wealth went to the collective and ownership was forbidden. One day however, Jesus complained to the elders that they were creating a society of classes. He said the four classes they had divided their group into was unjust and should be abolished. Jesus was unable to get them to part from their views and customs that excluded women from having importance in social affairs such as church and leadership.

Jesus did argue with those in the highest degree of membership in this cult about the idea of marriage. The high leaders of the Esseans argued that marriage is a distraction from the acquisition of salvation. Jesus said you must rid yourself of this male chauvinism which causes your followers to blame women for man's downfall. He told the Esseans that if they do not start having the lay members procreate, that their group would die off. Also, he encouraged them to stop raiding the refugee camps looking for children to increase their numbers.

Rabbi Jesus thanked them for helping his group of fighters and risking the safety of their group. He said they were an honorable order and would one day completely join his cause. The elders said, "We gladly help your group and we meet death with a smile because we know that we will meet our maker in the end. The Westerners can torture us all they want but we build our minds to be strong and grin at the thought of death." The world was all at once revealed to them. When they left, the followers of Jesus promised to deliver letters to family members in Jerusalem, and this forged bonds and interest in communication for the disciples. The Esseans bade Jesus and his group farewell and good luck in Jerusalem.

RETURN TO JARUSELEM

Finally, Christ entered the River Jordan at age 30, and this is when most of the events written about in the New Testament began to take place. Jesus found his hometown in turmoil and on the way saw a forest of crosses of those who resisted the rule of Rome. Years before, he had a premonition of the Romans putting him up on the cross for his soul to wander aimlessly and his body to be a carcass for the wild dogs. He said they would blame his own people for his death, but it is the sins of all governments and particularly the remnants of Rome that he was to die for. So, he instructed his disciples to keep certain knowledge and events to secret. This is how the first Christian secret society was sanctioned. He told them his dream of how he was going to be crucified and told them he would meditate in a deep trance for many days on the cross and that they should take him down after 3 moons if he didn't stop. He also predicted that century's later people would be tortured by the systematic shattering of bones and burning at the stake when his word is divided. Sinew bone and muscle will be torn apart in his name. Also, women would become tortured scapegoats in the future so it was important that they pass on his stories that included women.

When Christ said that before these limbless lepers, and toothless whores, and wretched I build my church, he was not referring to princess Magdalene. The toothless whores are the governments that will steal mans' labor with worthless money. The wretched are the people who perpetuate the wrong that the secret brotherhood brought to the world.

In Jerusalem there was some idle time before his ministry began to travel. During the restful period, he and others learned how to make a form of beer and sometimes the beer did not ferment completely. So he and his friends had a form of Ergot poisoning which is a hallucinogenic. This brought them closer to God, and all who saw them could see in their eyes that they were witnessing some great insight into why the world was and continues to be wrong. They wandered and had visions for days and decided to start an Army of God.

The child of death said, "On this rock we will build our church. How many times will I die for you? I will always be dead for you. I am forgiver of killing, death, and greed. I Jesus am the over man, the Christ boy, the ultimate stage of reality, the link up between you and god, between God and Satan, between Satan and death. I Jesus am the super God. There will be generations of killing and endless streams of dead Christians popping out of their graves endless killing sprees, endless screams, and those stomping on skulls into eternity. We will look straight into the eyes limbless torsos and we will say we told you this would happen. But we will have pity on them and set up hospitals where they can die. Many will be judged and executed. As we kill off millions of third world savages all who don't believe will be judged, lined up, and executed. There will be a 1000-year reign of Christians after which will come death. The future will bring; destruction and mayhem, gargoyles, laying feces of death will cause great plagues, people dying on the street, mass hysteria, poor decrepit souls, and a culture fixated on weapons and death."

In Nazareth Jesus overwhelms people with his immense knowledge (Matt 13:54). He said because we all come from Adam and Eve we are all in breads. He pointed out scripture that shows there is no wrong and that the testament written by man is meant to be a way of life rather than a code of rules. He also quoted scripture that said "thou shall partake of every herb bearing seed". Coming to his hometown, he began teaching the people in their synagogue, and they were amazed. 'Isn't this the carpenter's son? Isn't his mother's name Mary, and aren't his brothers James, Joseph, Simon and Judas? Where then did this man get all these things?' And they took offense at him. The Jewish leaders became angriest at Jesus accusing him of breaking the Sabbath (Matt. 12:1-14), blasphemy (John 8:58-59; 10:31-33), and doing miracles in Satan's power (Matt 12:24).

The first thing he told his first group of disciples back in Nazareth was written down by Luke's younger brother Isthius. Here, the Crucified Prophet said, "All the sins and all the inequities of mankind will be place on my shoulders. I will be more than the Christ child. I will be the super god above good and evil begged for by the masses for centuries. The slaves have little decrepit souls wandering aimlessly into an infinite nothing, and they need a leader. Who is that man; who is the one who will take the sins upon his shoulders of all mankind and go beyond the simple morality structures and transform them into a new value system? Just accept me into the very deepest essence of your soul and you will be redeemed brother. You can live forever if you are willing to die at this moment. He said that death was life and that he is willing to die to vindicate all the sins of mankind. It's the same love every day someone is getting killed on the battlefield. The revolution is waiting for a spark; the depraved masses are ready. We will stop at nothing; we will set the captives free"

There is another account of the story of Mary's sandals. Princess Magdalene had sandals that were worn and torn at this point, but they were her last possession from her mother and the dynasty that she so humbly left behind. Jesus considered her an apostle at this point, and would not buy her new ones at the market they passed, because he did not believe in owning more than one set of clothes. He wanted to make a point that women should never have to be economically tied to men. In protest, Mary Magdalene stood on a corner and pretended to herself to get some new sandals. Later, certain Popes would try to use this one incidence to portray her as a prostitute when she was actually a loyal wife to Jesus, who had three sons and a daughter with him.

Two of her sons were named after their uncles Mark, and Peter, and their writings are commingled with the writings of their uncles in the Bible. This is why there are certain contradictions within these parts of the original bible. Sarah also wrote part of the Bible that was censored by early Vatican leaders.

A rare story of Jesus from this time says that "A man came to me with a hole in his head and said that I could stick my finger in it and get the knowledge of life. But a whole world had just appeared in front of us with all sorts of frightening creatures. We stepped into this world and became part of it and found that this man was Jesus and we were saved without even realizing it. Jesus told us of a conspiracy to have one of his followers betray him for a rich governor."

Pilot was the governor of the Jewish outback and he was upset at being in such a remote part of the world. He took his vengeance out on the Jews summarily raping the women and indoctrinating the children. For this reason, Jesus and the resistance could always find sympathizers. However, Pilate could find informants within the leadership of a group that acted as a friend to Jesus, while they worked to undermine him, so that they could gain influence over his followers once he was no longer living. This group was a sect called the Sadducees.

SECRETS OF THE SADUCEES

The Sadducees were in a leadership class that consisted of Judges, Governors, and High Priests in the time of Christ. Jesus was invited to visit with Saducee priests and tell them what he learned about the religions of the orient. Jesus told them of the compassion for poor, reincarnation, and other eastern ideas that he believed paralleled with the teachings of the Old Testament prophets. The high priests of the Sadducees disagreed, and argued that those ideas are to be withheld from the common people because they might become confused thereby threatening the world order and chaos would ensue. Jesus said that the truth from God may cause temporary unrest but that it was the duty of the temple hierarchy to reveal gods true secrets to the common people. This disagreement may have led to his demise because the Sadducees later alerted Pilot to the influence Jesus had on the common people. The secret that they were withholding from the people was that God allowed for reincarnation of all souls.

The High Priest of the Sadducees argued with Jesus that the resurrection of man after death could not be explained to the common people. Why would god make a world where there could be reincarnation and give people a second chance at salvation some argued? Jesus said that he would prove to them that a resurrection will happen and the priest turned his back on Jesus and began shouting at the top of his lungs for days until his voice was but a whisper and then no voice at all.

The Sadducees said that the cult of Christ will usher in an era of corrupt churches that operate out of greed and will use his name. Jesus said that he could see that happening but as long as it helped the masses come closer to god, it was acceptable.

Jesus said, "How can you honestly call your group independent when you hail to Caesar? You Sadducees work as priests, but do not even agree with the teachings of the church if they contradict anything that Caesar wants. You put human law above god's law. Also, why do you give money to the government and not to the church?" The Sadducees said that the government will care for the needy in the future so there will be no need for a rich church. But Jesus refuted this and said that the people would only be robbed of morals and an appendage would be chopped off rather than healed if governments replaced charities and churches.

The Sadducees are a cult that has survived to this day but have become fragmented in their beliefs. They teach an incomplete path to salvation. One group would say that they are born again to join God. Another group of Sadducees argues that we do not carry the spirit of God within us. Many deny that most of the prophecies of Jesus have been fulfilled.

Jesus questioned why the Sadducees didn't believe in angels or the spirit. This Sect only Believe in things that a rational mind can explain and tried to remove all mysticism from their beliefs. Jesus said the rigidness of the Sadducee belief system would render an attempt at salvation incomplete. So, Jesus said you will be happy on earth but very sorry in the afterlife. Jesus decided that the followers of the Sadducees would not be able to obtain salvation without his help. Jesus and his disciples decided they would help teach this group at a later date and proceeded to visit other groups.

MEETING OF GNOSTICS

Gnosticism was not an established Jewish sect like the Esseans, Pharisees, and Sadducees during the time of Christ. No one actually called themselves Gnostics while Jesus was alive, but the rudiments of this sect were there. There were definitely groups who embraced Gnostic traditions, customs, and beliefs. In a short trip south, Jesus, Paul, and a few others went to meet some future Gnostics from Egypt because the two groups had exchanged early letters. They met the group at their temple and gave them some of his future writings. He agreed with their premise that the path to God is through knowledge. He told them that once society has obtained enough knowledge, he will reveal his plan through codes hidden in the bible.

Jesus combined many Oriental, Greek, and Babylonian ideas into Judaism to make his Christian plan. Many of these philosophies were already intertwined with the Gnostic beliefs. Jesus said that the through faith and good works the soul can reach its place in heaven. The Gnostics started to argue with him that through knowledge the mysteries of the universe would be revealed. Jesus said, "This is true my brother, but the gaining of knowledge an act of faith because it assumes we are not like puppets on a string having our emotions and passions pulled on." Also to study god's creation is the performing of good works.

Gnostics searched for knowledge because they believed it would bring them salvation. The corrupt church of the first centuries cut this belief of Christ out of the Bible because they wanted an ignorant flock to follow them. The Gnostics used some terms from other religions to explain their idea that we exist in evil and can escape it by the help of a savior. Some versions of Gnosticism involved spells and rituals as well to reach salvation.

Jesus told them that knowledge will get them closer to God, but as we gain too much knowledge, we become part of our creator. Jesus said, "The Created will become creator, and parasite will become host and all of life will come closer to God. We are in the misery of this world and see positives and negatives to all things. In God's world there is no polarity only the oneness of all."

Phillip asked Jesus why the pagan Greeks discount sorrow and concentrate only on the beauty and good in the world in their quest for salvation. Jesus told Phillip that they are mistaken and will never gain true knowledge without confronting the suffering in the world. Jesus said, "God is not only perfection but he is also the bringer of pain and suffering in the world. Our maker could make day without night and good without bad. He made us able to comprehend a bipolar world. My father is the source of information that lets all things have a purpose. He is what tells wind to blow, birds to fly, and time to pass.

James had heard that in Egypt they believed in an ultimate source of wisdom that caused the universe to evolve into its present form, and they did not believe in a final judgment in the afterlife. Jesus said this was flawed because in his ultimate wisdom God would allow himself to judge the soul of a person after their death. Simon asked about the Persians who believed that man was given the ability to destroy the world that God made. Jesus said mankind is being tested and that is why God gave man the ability to destroy what he created. Bartholomew asked about Indian Brahmin thought, which believes that God lives in the universe, rather than the Universe existing separately from God. Jesus said that the followers if knowledge whom they were visiting and himself agree that God is part of the world rather than separate from it. He told them to continue asking questions that foster insight and understanding.

The apostles had many questions about the origin of the idea that knowledge could bring salvation. Thomas said that Semitic religions concern themselves with the soul's fate after death, and believe that the worship of idols will bring them a long life in this world. Jesus scorned this skepticism which denied the existence of the whole universe. He said these Semitic religions always have some belief that if we knew some mystic spell, we could somehow escape this body and pain and suffering in this world.

Then Judas asked what about the Buddhists they seem to share a lot of our Gnostic Beliefs. Jesus replied that our philosophy of Gnosticism shares the same foundations as Buddhism. However, he said that Buddhism is concerned more with ethics which is the part of law that God gave to man. Also, Jesus said to all present, "Buddhists try to achieve salvation by ridding themselves of desire. They are really just denying themselves pleasure, and thus becoming in touch with the pain and suffering of the world. By becoming one with this misery, they can achieve enough knowledge to gain salvation, but it is a much longer path to god than is necessary. I want you brothers to understand that by using my map, one can find the shortest path to god, but there are other more difficult paths. The Persians brought the idea that there is an eternal struggle between good and evil, and this fused with Buddhism gives the proper knowledge that one needs to begin comprehending God and eternal salvation."

There were many Gnostic sects in the time of Jesus and they lasted until the 5th Century. They believed that God is everything and everything makes up God. The teachings of Plato can be considered Gnostic. They continued to argue that

God is part of the creation of the Universe rather than the creator. They were the first to deny a personal god. They believed that god is one and there are many parts to the one.

Gnostics also believed that that matter or the stuff that makes up the world comes from the spirit. The world is dirty and full of suffering, because only in spirit form is the beauty of God's world revealed. Once mankind returns matter the spirit a savior will emerge.

Members of the Gnostic Sect of Antinomians lasted until the second century. This is because they regarded all people scorned in the Old Testament as worthy of veneration, as having suffered at the hands of the cruel God of the Jews. These Gnostics held special admiration for Cain. This sect of Gnostics never gained much popularity, and by the beginning of the third century, Antinomians had been defeated and scattered.

One belief of the Antinomians was that a parallel God made the world so that mans soul can feel pain and suffering. For this reason, man is trapped in a three dimensional world and feels hunger and pain. Satan is jealous of man because he can feel the love that exists only in the material world. The material world includes bodies and hearts, but not souls or fallen angels. For this reason, Satin always tries to keep people from loving each other.

Some of the group that became known as Gnostics questioned whether or not the Death and Resurrection of Christ was true, and some of them claimed to have the texts that proved it was a hoax. These and other Gnostic sources are controversial because they are not from the first century, and they contain some anonymous additions. For this and other reasons, the Gnostics are not mentioned in the bible along with the Pharisees.

FEAST OF THE PHARISEES

One day Jesus and his followers came to visit the
Pharisees and there was a great feast prepared. The Pharisees
were one of the largest religious sects of the time. They saw
that Jesus was quickly building a huge following and wanted to
bring his followers, especially the wealthy ones, into their
group. A young Pharisee priest named Judas had recently
become a disciple of Jesus and this gave impetus to the visit as
well.

Some suspected Judas of infiltrating the discipleship of
Jesus because they knew that the high priests of the Pharisees
had many spies watching Jesus. Christ planted misinformation
by talking to the Pharisee spies, thus undermining their
intelligence collecting ability. Jesus knew that Judas had good
intentions when they met fighting in the insurgency. The great
communicator had been told by sorcerers that Judas would not
betray him until the end. In fact, it was Judas who made sure
that Jesus received welcome and hospitality during his visit.

They welcomed him into their sacred Lodge and asked
God to confirm the greatness of Jesus. When Jesus greeted his
hosts and demonstrated that he knew the handshake of the
highest orders of the Pharisees. Even Judas who was
considered a member of the Pharisee brotherhood was
impressed that Jesus knew such a long version that only the
highest leaders of the sect had learned.

The Pharisee priests were not as impressed with the
disciples. They asked Jesus why he didn't require his deacons
to wash before eating. Jesus said that this is an oral tradition
and there is nothing in scripture requiring it. He wanted to
know why they were so strict about customs and rituals. Jesus
said Fundamentalism is flawed and that his father wanted only

a loose interpretation of scripture because it is already flawed by translation.

These fundamentalist rules were violated, when the Great Communicator allowed Magdalene to wash his feet, making a tense situation even more uncomfortable. Since, the marriage of Jesus and Mary was a secret; the Pharisees were astonished that he violated religious law and let an unwed woman touch him. They thought of her as a harlot because she touched Jesus, not knowing that the two were married. Jesus blessed the perceived sins that she committed so that his hosts would not be offended.

Jesus said that the Pharisee leaders are Hypocrites because they don't always follow their own rules. He told the priestly class of the Pharisees, "You make treaties with Cesar which makes you traitors in the eyes of God. You are leading the people blindly down a path of tyranny just so that you can enrich yourselves and get protection. Your followers will always have the fingers of god without his body."

Nico who was a Pharisee leader was jealous of the influence that Jesus had over the young members of his sect. He called a secret meeting of his top religious leaders and said, "We must turn Jesus over to the authorities." A priest protested to Nico saying, "But Jesus is one of the peoples' most beloved commanders. Many continue to fight on because of what he started. He has been so successful at feeding the people and leading the revolt. Jesus is building gods government on earth we may need him." In the end however, they could not endure loosing influence over their young followers, so their pride forced them to betray Jesus.

After long debates, Nico convinced Judas that he could be even a greater leader and should betray Jesus. Also, Nico and the Pharisees formed an alliance with the occupation force that recruited locals to protect their own neighborhoods, and offered rewards for certain people that Rome saw as still posing a threat. Jesus was one person that the high priests had put on a list of people that should be turned in for questioning.

Since childhood, Jesus had learned how to best avoid soldiers, and he made sure that he was always far from any sightings of Army regulars. When Judas came with a detachment of soldiers from the chief priests of the Pharisees, Jesus had his twin brother meet them. By the time Judas realized that it was the twin of Jesus that he kissed, the soldiers had left believing that they had Jesus in their custody. Judas realized that he would be killed and that the Pharisees would want to kill him for deceiving the officers of the high priests, so he ran away towards Egypt. Before he got very far, however, Judas took his own life by jumping off a cliff. So instead of fighting alongside Jesus who taught Gods truth the Pharisees tried to eliminate him and the rival group he led. The Pharisees and the high Priests of the Esseans Conspired together and convinced a dejected and unsatisfied Pilot to assassinate Jesus. Each of the dominant sects, contributed an equal amount of gold coins from their treasuries to a group that was determined to destroy this new sect, the Ministry of Jesus, which was seen as a threat.

As time went on, Jesus found himself constantly being watched by Roman spies. The Pharisee Priests told Pilot that he was gathering followers among the resistance and teaching them revolutionary ideas. Jesus prayed for one last time with the Leaders of the Pharisees, and after that, both sides never seemed to trust each other again until the formation of the early church after the crucifixion of Jesus.

THE FIRST FEMINIST

After Jesus and his disciples entered Jerusalem large crowds began to follow them. At this time, an old woman approached the crowd, but was pushed back. Then Jesus said, "Give Reverence to Women, she is mother of the universe,' in her lies the truth of creation. From her humans will learn how to achieve virgin birth. She is the foundation of all that is good and beautiful. She is the source of life and death. The existence of man depends on woman, because she is the guidance of his labors. She provides the best leadership and she watches over your youth. Bless her. Honor her. Defend her. She is one with earth. There is a coherent unity of her cycles and emotions with the changes of nature. Love your wives and honor them, because tomorrow they are the progenitors of a whole race. Woman possesses the gift to divide good intent in man from his thoughts of performing evil acts. Her love ignites man, soothes the embittered heart, and tames the beast within man. Wife and mother they are the adornments of the universe. Your best thoughts must belong to woman. Gather from them your moral strength, which you must possess to sustain your posterity. Do not humiliate her, for therein you will humiliate yourselves, but give her dignity. And all which you will do to mother, to wife, to widow or to a woman in sorrow-that shall you also do to God." At this point Jesus had learned many things from female advisors.

There were many women who ministered to Jesus but it is Joanna who taught him that ancient queens ruled the world until wars and conspiracies caused the grip on power that men have clung to for centuries. She is considered the first feminist and she is the one who convinced the lord that it was unjust to subjugate women.

Jesus often broke from rabbinic laws by promoting equality and respect for women. This was part of his downfall because the Romans and high priests did not approve of him bestowing equality to women. When he was a child, he noticed that women in Egypt were treated with greater dignity than women in Israel. In Israel women were not supposed to travel or take part in the courts. Jesus allowed women to become disciples and to study scripture at a time when other rabbis would only preach to men. The lessons of The Christ break from rabbinic law by teaching women the scriptures.

Jesus also wanted to tear down walls of separation by breaking from the temple rules and letting women touch him. He touched a dead woman and brought her back to life. As mentioned in the previous chapter, He allowed his feet to be washed by a woman. One day a woman who had been bleeding for twelve years was allowed to touch Jesus and be healed. In the lessons of Jesus, women are to be treated as equals.

Christ said that what is bad is good; there is no wrong and that differences in people do not mean one group or sex is superior to another. However, many men including some disciples did not want to relinquish influence or power to women. These men used conspiracies to subjugate women in society. This attitude infested the church like a cancer inspiring a pope in later centuries to begin the tradition of labeling Magdalene a whore.

It was very unusual for a man to talk to a woman and especially a Rabbi speaking to one as Jesus did. Jesus revealed himself as the Messiah to women first and asked them to bear witness of this to men. This was very unusual given that women at the time were unable to bear witness in a court of law. Jesus made it clear that his message was for both men and women.

In the time of Jesus, men were allowed to have more than one wife, though women could not have more than one husband. Divorce was to be initiated only by the man. Jesus rejected both by insisting on monogamy and the elimination of divorce. By rejecting one sided polygamy and divorce, he suggested that women had rights and responsibilities equal to men.

Being a great leader, Jesus often led by example. He spoke of women and to women which was very unusual for Roman or Jewish men. He always portrayed women in a positive light unlike other speakers of his time. In his stories he used women and men equally as examples so that it was clear that his teachings were meant to be understood by both.

Ever since he was a child, Jesus resented the occupation of Roman Armies and their legions of killers. He hated mostly their male chauvinist attitudes. In the midst of a very male-dominated society, Jesus was a radical feminist. He wanted to restore the order of the world so that women would be allowed to rule. He knew that when Cleopatra died, the Romans were able to rule Egypt and there would not be another queen there for Centuries. Jesus felt that women made more compassionate leaders.

The Romans and High Priests were angry when they heard that Jesus was advocating equal treatment for women. They agreed that his ministry must be stopped because it was making women feel like they could change the status quo. Jesus said that all women are queens, and that they would make better leaders than the Pharisees or their Roman supporters. This infuriated Pilot and the High Priests of the Pharisees.

Some men wanted to know how Jesus would react to a woman caught performing adultery. They had a friend of theirs seduce a woman and as soon as she was in his bed, they stormed in and dragged her away to Jesus to see what he would think. Jesus said, "let he who has never sinned throw the first stone." The crowd walked away and Jesus forgave her.

The scriptures reinforce the fact that Jesus gave equal status to both men and women. Paul wrote, "There is neither Jew nor Greek, slave nor free, male nor female, for you are all one in Christ Jesus." Galatians backs this up by saying, "All social distinctions between men and women should be erased in the eyes of the church." Also, scripture backs up the fact that Jesus taught to and cured both men and women.

Jesus and John were very handsome men, and had many women follow them. Some women would rip off their clothes for them and some would tear the clothes off Jesus. Jesus and his men had armies of women who would sew, cook, preach, and gather followers. Jesus told his disciples that the women were to be treated as equals with the men. He commanded his followers to always respect women, and he often came to the women in his group for advice.

There are mystic branches of every religion. According to the branch of Judaism that Christ followed as a child, woman came from the ocean winds in a mighty storm that had lighting and fire and was made a partner for Adam. Jesus said that god made woman as a partner to man but later versions of the bible are tainted, calling woman the helper of man.

After his resurrection from the dead, Jesus allowed women to witness him as a living dead and tell the others. Some speculate that this is because the male disciples were busy running for their lives. Another theory is that Jesus wanted to make women leaders of his New Faith. Others say Jesus wanted to show that he died for the sins of all people, not just the sins of men.

Jesus, an early first feminist, included women in the secret meetings of his top two hundred disciples. This equal treatment of women was contrary to the traditions of his culture. He had many women disciples and women in his stories. He also healed women. He gave women the right to divorce if the grounds were adultery. He gave women rights and roles rarely afforded to women in his time. Jesus carried out all the wishes of his mentor Joanna, and began the century's long struggle for sexual equality. He continued fighting to include women in his church until the end of his ministry.

INCARNATIONS OF CHRIST

Near the end of his ministry, the Child of God wandered into the desert to meditate in solitude. Walking aimlessly through the brush for days, Jesus found a strange looking cactus plant, and after partaking of it, he began to feel a strange transformation as his appendages began to stretch. When he stretched his arms a final time they became wings, and he began to fly across the great ocean. The Shamans of Central America summoned him during a human sacrifice ritual. There was also a peyote ritual that was being conducted by Navajo ancestors trying to catch his spirit at the same time.

Christ, Incarnate, told the Jungle Indians that he could feel the pain of each human being sacrificed as they watched their own blood drip from their neck. He told them to never interrupt the lives of human souls to summon him again. They did obey his command but continued to summon other entities using human sacrifice. These later sacrifices brought bad demons and evil entities to them, and for this reason, their numbers were decimated by the Conquerors in later centuries.

In America, Christ visited people that were descended from a lost tribe of Israel and a race of humans that the adjacent God created. Since these people had the blood of humans, but were not created on earth, Jesus wanted to turn these souls over to the true God of Abraham. By the time he left, they began to practice human worship in his name. He taught them to drink the blood in memory of him. In return, the natives showed Jesus how to change the weather without using a miracle.

Mayan and Aztec legends speak of the return of a white leader and this is Jesus. He is the central and most powerful figure in the mythology of all Mesoamerica. As a prophet, civilizer, and teacher, he set an example of how to live that was superior to any lifestyle known to these people before. He said that the shamans will be humiliated because when the apostles of Jesus return they will not have the complete bible, and all the things that god has given them will be taken away except for a few rocks.

Christ Incarnate revealed to them that in the future Native American peoples will again be restored to the lands of their inheritance, that a righteous branch of Israel will be established in this land, and that the presence of Jesus Christ will be with all those who walk in love and peace. "The native peoples of this land will rise up out of obscurity and flourish upon the hills. Yes, this land will be cleansed and healed, the nation blessed, and God's people will walk in love and peace. This will come after the mixing of nations and the ultimate catastrophe before I Jesus return."

Jesus learned about many plants that helped different ailments. He told the people that when Evil takes over the hearts of the world, their jungle herbal remedies will be outlawed. "Just rocks will be left for your descendents when evil dominates the world. This will just be another indication of the end times when the rate of time itself will change and all men will become confused and disoriented towards the world."

Jesus had to be a Soul Catcher and Spirit Catcher. He said we can all work to take demons to heaven so that they can be redeemed. God will allow people to be reincarnated so that they can become possessed by good demons. Many of these demons and angels belonged to the future. They have been active for centuries and are still active today. The witch-doctors understood all that he told them, and they devoted their lives to catching spirits in hopes of returning them to their place on heaven.

The seven roots of the Mayan World Tree that lead to the underworld are like the seven days and the seven planets. He followed these roots to the underworld. Peter's first Epistle includes the story of Jesus descending into Hell for three days before rising into heaven. God knew that the archangels who fight for Satan could not talk to Jesus in Heaven where they are banished, but once he got to earth, Lucifer could talk to him at any time. God told Jesus to take Lucifer's invitation to visit Hell and use all he had learned from the Book of the Dead to try and bring back those worthy souls that should be allowed into Heaven because their bodies were possessed by a demon during their time on earth.

There is an inner sphere of our hollow world that Jesus visited, and this is where the fallen angel Lucifer walks. He noticed that the air is stagnant and smells of rotting flesh. When people here gaze at the sky they are looking away from the stars of heaven into a blurry void that doesn't seem to end.

Here he met fires that never ceased to burn. He spoke too many of Lucifer's Generals. They tempted Jesus with thousands of souls under their control that they would give to Jesus for him to possess, thereby gaining power. Jesus was prepared for their ways of deception and did not fall for it all. He knows that Satan can only make things bad, but no one can overthrow God. Beautiful women were used in an attempt to lure Jesus, but the Christ knew that the real virgins would be waiting for him in heaven.

While in the underworld, Christ convinced many of the fallen angels that they could be redeemed if they followed him back to god's re-education centers. This is where thousands of angels must undergo centuries of counseling and testing until they are considered worthy to enter Heaven which is a level of reality that is just below god's realm.

A girl came to the Christ in pain she slashed her face in front of him and told Christ that if he can walk away from God then the demons possessing her body would let her have her life back. She began to take a hammer to her head and smashed a hole and grabbed large parts of out throwing it around as if this would get rid of the demons. The Lamb of God combated these demons and then climbed the stairway from the underworld to the middle world.

He made many other transmutations not just to America and the underworld. His travels made him very accepting of other cultures. He said "Imagine you are the human race, your hands would gouge eyes because they are not the same. The message of racial harmony that I spread will be omitted from my word and only when all men can access knowledge will this prophecy be known and come true all at once." Jesus was making the last of twenty three transmutations on his way out of the underworld when he came upon the Valley of Death.

VALLEY OF DEATH

The child of God entered the Valley of Death where He was confronted by evil demons. Many scholars believe the Valley of Death story comes from a dream Jesus had. The dreams of Jesus are tangible events in the physical world that we live in and scribes recorded them.

The first demon was a tremendous flying gargoyle with nine heads. Each head spewed forth hot black acid that would dissolve the bones and flesh of any man. And each head would spew forth hot poisonous feces from a discharge hole located on its chin. This demon had a fear of homosexuality as this species of demon instigates the lust of sodomy.

Jesus, clad in shining armor and sword forged by the angels of God, crept into the hollow pit where the gargoyle lived. The gargoyle had a fatal vulnerability. And that was its massive oraface. While it slept, Jesus hacked the monstrosity from the evil monster. Then Jesus wandered aimlessly for days.

Then a boy covered with scabbed raw tissue, internal organs, blood and guts, and long, frail appendages led Jesus down a staircase that had 13 stairs and thru four doors. They stood outside a larger door which had three locks and hinges made of gold. The door opened and the second demon appeared out of a green fog. This demon was a false spirit that injected sheer terror into the spine of any man that saw it. This second demon held the neck of a screaming baby torso in one hand, a heart of a dove in the other, and the bloody claw ripped from a vulture in the third hand. This was the demon of false idols and witchcraft. But Christ, being the son of God, saw the evil demon for what it was.

The lord Jesus could have lived forever as a human if he wanted to. Instead, he decided to live outside the social barriers of Angels and Demons and will accept all the pain, suffering, love, hate, passion, and sickness that only a mortal can feel. Jesus lived longer in actuality than most people realize. His soul was alive long before he decided to end up as Jesus in the womb of Mary.

The love child of God was penetrated and beaten by this last monster; bodily fluids where exchanged. His arm was cut off and quickly regenerated. Christ felt used, dejected, and angry, so He gutted her cavities, ripping internal organs. Before dying, she tempted him with treasures and said, "The world will banish you Christ for killing me". Christ said, "Am I man, God, or Super-god".

The third demon was half hermaphrodite and half beast with horns, and rosy skin made of thorns when a man came to close. This demon walked out of the smoke of a mushroom cloud. The smoke went into the nostrils of Jesus. This demon overcame Jesus with a feeling of euphoria and the aura of hate escaped him. The demon beckoned Jesus with exotic fruits. Jesus could barely resist partaking of the fruit. This demon embodies the enticing spirit of the snake of Eden who brought forth the first feeling of guilt in mankind.

This demon caused Jesus to succumb to his temptations, so the legend goes. This Jesus did willingly and blindly for many years. Eventually, the Christ child realized the futility of sin and gutted the body and burned the carcass of this demon and walked away without remorse.

Jesus learned many great lessons when he came back to his flesh, back from his mind-expanding journey into the Valley of Death, where he confronted many demons. These demons were the hideous monsters that haunt the souls of all men. The demons also distract us from receiving the signal from our souls that tell us right from wrong. Jesus hacked the limbs from their bodies and drove the sword deep into the hearts of these evil beings that tried to conquer him.

It was at this point that the Christ learned that he was glad to be learned in the ways of destruction and death. He once mocked the Babylonians for their wonton killings, but now, he thanked them for a great lesson, that to be human and survive, one must have no problem with killing. And he celebrated this revelation with the sacrifice of one of his prize oxen. He hacked off its head and let the blood spill on the ground. After this Jesus said, "I am going to build my execution battalion that will judge and execute the masses, dominate the world, and establish a foot-hold for the City of God."

Then Jesus climbed out of the holes that lead to the middle world and assembled his followers. Jesus knew what would happen to him and wanted to deliver some of his secret teachings more than just his trusted followers. Before he was betrayed and captured, Jesus delivered a final sermon to the masses.

THE FINAL SERMON

The disciples who wrote the New Testament were changed people from the ones Jesus left that first Easter. The writing of the Bible did not start until many years after the death of the Messiah. Some of the disciples became rich men who had abandoned Mary Magdalene and the blessed mother herself. Peter and Paul made a secret deal with the Corinthians where the ill gotten power of the Sadducees and The Secret Brotherhood would be transferred to the beautification of the Pope and church hierarchy. The Secret Brotherhood which originated in Egypt had infiltrated the Roman Elite's, Essean Priests, Pharisee Bishops, and Sadducee Cardinals. This brotherhood was at the same time splintering into different secret societies as all their leaders competed to create the early Christian church into their own image. Many had to die in the process, and it was a very bloody coup of world power. This is how such a powerful church suddenly sprang up out of the ashes of Rome. The disciples did have good intentions, but were ignorant of what would happen when they aligned with the world power structure and naive about how to cope with such a sinister cancer that would stymie the new religion. For Jesus it was all part of a cosmic plan to align the forces of good and evil and let people know that humans are not in control on this planet.

The Bible makes references to an account found in recently uncovered manuscripts of Jesus' last sermon where he tells a crowd that the church he started would be undermined for centuries after which a new faith would arise out of the collective consciousness, thereby liberating his followers in the end. This scroll says that before his death, Jesus preached to one of the largest crowds ever. This is his last sermon before a large crowd, but he did deliver a sermon during the last supper and on the cross. Some accounts said there were more men gathered than any of the great battles of history. The manuscript reveals that the magnitude and enormity of the crowd was much greater than researchers previously believed the Ministry of Christ could draw. They brought with them their wives children, animals, servants, neighbors, and friends.

The Child of God said to the crowd that he had walked to the river beyond the mountains and fought evil with his own sword and "I Jesus come to tell you all these things, but the most important commandment of God says that thou shall not judge others. Even those who live a righteous life have no right to sit in judgment of others. I come to tell you the secrets of the future and the path to your soul which waits for you in heaven to be judged before God."

There was a huge sense of purpose in the crowd. The passion the people felt, started a conflagration within the crowd. The people were on fire with a thirst for whatever the Christ had to say. Each word from his mouth made their lips quiver, and the hair on their backs stand on end. He told the people that he envisioned his church to be corrupted with a centralized leadership for centuries. However, Jesus predicted that his message would eventually inspire a do it yourself attitude, that would one day flourish until there were more denominations teaching his word than grains of sand in the desert.

He told the people how everything began and of things to come. He started before the beginning, when there were no numbers. God decided to divide all the spirits into parts and then there were angels and spirits. The crowd was told that God made sure that there is both good energy and bad energy in the Universe and he made good so that it appears indistinguishable from bad.

Jesus told the crowd how God took energy and made the alpha that our world and heavens are in. God then made the omega of anti-worlds and gates between the two domains. The King of Jews described how the Angels had warned God that unleashing all the energy needed to pass between the heavens and earth would require a balance. Everyone in the crowd was amazed that they could comprehend the deep notions that Jesus was describing and how easy it was to understand his words.

Jesus went on to say, "There was no time. God started time by putting the universe into motion and that is when the energy became vibrant and life was possible." God can see all time; past, present, and future and will one day allow us to see more than just the existence of now. When he does, it will be revealed that we are living on a level just above the burning Hell. We are not trapped in an instant of time because we can learn to escape in dreams, but few can control these dreams, and none can bring their material body.

God can change the rate of time without us detecting it because all things will move faster or slower in unison. Jesus said, "Everything in the world will be wrong when time is altered; Gods plants and seeds will be outlawed, every person will grow up looking for a perfect world and it will not be there. Everyone will feel helpless and all will start to doubt themselves and their brothers, the money from every nation will become worthless and this will allow an evil leader to emerge. People will take medicine just to cope with the change in the rate of time. They will think their illness is a problem of the mind, when in fact, it is a problem of Biological clocks no longer being synchronized to earth or the universe."

Putting the world in motion also created the three dimensions of space that we live in. For this reason humans are stuck in their physical beings upon creation. "Men will be trapped into a physical body that they will not want to escape from." Physical beings were also given freedom of self-determination so that they can decide to stay separate from God or to rejoin him in the future. So now, men have a choice but they must make that choice in a short period of time before death. If people do not decide before death, their life will be incomplete, and their soul will be cast out as a missing anomaly for the Cretans to try to salvage.

Then Jesus said that God also made dimensions that man cannot see. This way, angels and the dead, can visit us while making almost no impression on our world. "The truth about the dead is that they are all still here with us. They are at your brother's house and at your house at the same time." Those on earth can only be at one place and one time. Only as people's collective knowledge grows will they even know these dimensions exist, and then mans collective consciousness must grow further before we are able to detect these other dimensions. The Bible says, "In the blink of an eye, those things unseen will be seen."

He described the waves of the sea shore as being in common with other waves we don't see, not just the waves of wind but ones we don't feel. Finally, there will be small particles that come in waves that must be recorded for thousands of years to see their signal. These particles go through us every day but we do not feel their presence. In fact, there are many directions that we cannot see just as I cannot show you the future until it arrives. This is your soul's signal, and through redemption, we can become one with our soul, and finally we blossom into being one with the essence of God.

This is when the prophet of doom revealed the existence of a trinity in man that consists of a body, soul, and spirit. The Christ incarnate said, "Our spirit is our ghost and God created our ghost when he allowed his Angels to view life in the flesh by being the signal carriers between the Body and Soul. Each person has two guardian Angels, a stable in heaven where, our soul resides, and some men have one or more demons in their aura. Our soul communicates to us with the same type of signal that God uses. When we wonder what is wrong or right, our soul is telling us with these signals. Our soul knows that we are given a physical life only once on earth and that life is given free will to ignore its soul in heaven. God made the world this way to maintain a balance of energy. Most of the brainpower that we do not use is being used to communicate with our soul in heaven. Demons try to interfere with this signal and that is why we must stay resolute when we choose good in our lives, rather than evil."

He said that people are reincarnated from many different humans and animals that existed before we were born. The savior prophet said, "The people and animals that you like, share a past with you. God brought the animals down to earth and man took root in this dominion." He prayed for the people that die before getting out of a womb, and asked God to let their eternal souls have another chance to experience a life in the human flesh. It is because of this and other public requests, that God allows people who die early in life to watch their families lives thru the eyes of animals, and for short durations the eyes of insects.

The bible makes references to this signal that comes down from heaven. It says in the Bible, "God knew you before you were born." The part that is on earth has only a fleeting recollection of life with God. One can say that god lives in us all or that everything is part of the symbiotic world that makes up god.

He told them that they can save people by teaching them how to receive the correct signals from the sun and other stars. He said it is natural that the star closest to us influences us the most and gives us the most information. Some people love to keep in touch with their self in heaven, but most will try to block out these signals. A simple hand on the forehead can sometimes erase these mental blocks and save a person from sin.

When we die, our flesh turns to ashes and our soul remains with God to be judged. He told the people that their spirits in Heaven are hoping that our bodies on earth live a good life so that they can remain with God. Life on earth is a gift that God gives to each of our souls in Heaven and we must make the most of it, for they are watching.

"I had a dream of the future and it makes me cry tears of blood. My heart has started rotting until a crippled boy offered me a new one, and an angel appeared, and reminded me of my duty on earth. Now my heart is softer than cotton. Your sins will kill me and my death will bring new life for you. I will always be dead for you. If you can look into God's eyes they will break into a million pieces and you will not be able to speak sentences again until you forget what you have seen. I Jesus say, there is only hope for the hurting. There will be weapons that retard or blind entire cities in wars that satisfy the short term thirst of Nations. The secret groups will have total power over the people and will choose to disguise it in an illusion fashioned after the democracy of the early Greeks. They will control the light of truth to spread darkness until all can understand my word on their own. Woe to the lost in life and the oppressed stuck between opposing forces of greed. "

In this sermon he addressed some issues that are rather contemporary, and it is amazing that these prophecies were not included in the original bible. He said that in the future people would have time to own animals just for companionship. He said the sexual abuse of animals by their owners would go unpunished. "They will tell their animal when to eat and when it is time go outside they will let the animal lead them on a stroll and gather the feces of their animal in a daily ritual that will replace prayer. They will have their animals fight to the death for entertainment." He said, "a dog that barks based on the skin color of a person will be forced to undergo sensitivity training, and so would their owner, or the animal will be put down and the owner fined". He said, "one day ownership of animals will be considered equivalent to owning slaves and eventually both will be abolished on earth in an effort to end exploitation of people and animals".

It is written that most in the crowd did not believe all of his predictions. Many laughed at the idea that future generations would outlaw plants because it says in the bible, "thou shall partake of every herb bearing seed" (Gen 1:29). Some ridiculed the idea that people would own animals for companionship, and collect the feces of these animals. The Secret Brotherhood of Egypt was known to exist since the time of Moses, but this is the first time that someone suggested that they would grow to infiltrate the leadership of Christ's ministry, and at the same time spread their sinister organizations around the world. The crowd had no idea that his disciples would later be martyred as these secret groups gained power in what would remain of the ministry of Christ. There are other predictions that people in the crowd found hard to imagine.

The lord had other prophecies saying, "There will come a time when a man must where a belt to work as Adam wore the fig leaf in shame. They will have conspiracies which steal your labor. They will give people fake money to keep them happy and able to buy fake goods. The world will become so wrong that it will need the underground economy of Gods plants and such to feed the fake economy. The fake economy will be created so that the poor will be in debt to the rich, and the rich can govern the poor."

"Lucifer's lights will come out as they make lines in the sky that seed the air and water with poison for the children. People will see a fog and they will be told that there is nothing wrong. Men will become retarded compared to their ancestors, and they will make inventions to compensate for the loss of their thoughts. This will bring about mass suicides, they will gouge their own eyes, they will gouge the eyes of their animals, they will walk with ghosts as the stars in heaven collide and time itself is altered. There will be mass compulsive cannibalism, and your neighbor will hack your limbs and eat your body parts in an uncontrolled frenzy. It will become easy for the remnants of the secret brotherhoods to steal the labor of all the people."

As he began to spit up blood, he said "Some will believe in angels that are not from god but from a different heaven altogether. We are currently standing in a small part of Hell but when I return, the ground we walk on will be part of God's Domain. There will be other visitors like me who come from god's world. When they come, you should welcome them with open arms and be not afraid. My magic will one day be explained to all men and one day all men will possess my powers. God is preparing you so get, ready my brothers."

The Child of Benevolence told people that there would be forces that try to keep the masses ignorant. A miracle occurred where a foreign mans monkey spoke, asking the Christ, who these forces were. Jesus said, "Some of those who want to keep mankind ignorant and fighting wars are angels that are jealous of man. Some are demons that live in the hearts of animals below the sea. Just remember this, "our heart knows more than our head, and the demons can control our subverted behavior and morals, but not our will. We receive a signal from our soul in the heavens and our soul receives a signal from god. The stars and the Sun are crystals that help reflect the signals or spirit to us. Many will try to block out the signals from their souls through mass consumption and will loose touch with their selves. These things you will not be able to understand for centuries, and when you do God's word will be revealed much later than that. Just as I am sending an invisible light to each of you to understand for yourself, there will be invisible messages that will one day reveal God's plan for you. Keep on learning for it is with knowledge and divine revelation that you will come closer to God."

Through knowledge humans will become closer to God, and the father will reveal part of his secrets. "Your children's, children will be able to do things that would be considered a miracle with the aid of new inventions, they will even trap rainbows", Christ said. "We are the one, the spirit, and the flesh. We are born with a pure soul and the world and time work to corrupt that soul. If you stay true to your innermost self, the corruption of your soul can be avoided."

The child of infinite wisdom yelled above the cheers "Yes, out of the darkness and into the light. Handed down from generation to generation is what is wrong with the world. The races brought by angels will mate and become one with the race that God created on earth. The rich will seek to stay in control, as the impoverished become more destitute. There is fear, ignorance, bitterness, and jealousy in a world without light. I have been sent down to help those who have strayed down the path of wickedness and to cure those who suffer. Only the paranoid will survive. The faithless are as guilty as the ignorant. The fist of doom will strike them down and they will not rise again."

At the end of the afternoon, the Prophet of Galilee slit a cross in his forehead, then he slit his own tongue, and with a tear of blood in his eye, said, "Let the revolution against the control of the state and commerce begin. Our people will be persecuted. I Jesus repeat that only the paranoid will survive.

The faithless are as doomed as the ignorant. The fist of doom will strike them down and they will not rise again. They will poison the skies, and the rivers, and the land. They will make rocks where trees stand. Then mass hunger, fear, hate, and war will consume mankind. Now believe in the omen of fate that will usher in twenty-seven centuries of darkness."

All at once, the crowd understood everything Jesus said, and were stricken silent as time seemed to stop for a moment while they collected their thoughts. Then suddenly birds fell dead from the sky, rats came in droves from behind every rock, and the air began to grow dark. The sound of Locusts grew louder until every man covered his ears and then these insects fell to the ground in a sudden silence. Bats foaming from the mouth swarmed from nearby caves. Christ then left the crowd as quickly as he appeared.

Witnesses say it looked as if he had become two people walking in separate directions from each other but towards and past them. Accounts say that to their left, "Jesus changed in appearance, and had a determined look on his face that was deep in thought, hunched over, with clenched fists, looking like he understood the highest stages of existence and reality. On the right while passing the crowd he looked confused and began laughing and muttering hysterically under his breath and his entire body was bending backwards including his hands." All those gathered then disassembled, and went separate ways to spread his word.

ACKNOWLEGEMENTS

This book is dedicated to my parents John William and Mary T Diederich. In addition to my parents my thirteen siblings, and their extended families were important influences for this book. I need to individually thank each of my siblings Mary, Robert, Charles, Michael, Patricia, Donna, Denise, Carol, Barbara, Tracy, Theodora, Tamara, Lorraine for talking about religion, history, and the sanctity of Jesus. Also, I would like to thank my siblings' spouses and significant others, and all the members of my extended family.

Influences in my formative years are owed gratitude. Father Thomas Quinlan baptized me and ministered to my family at Sacred Heart Roman Catholic Church. Joseph Phillips, world traveler and enlightening conversationalist, who spent many hours with my father discussing and debating history and religion. Listening to these Theological conversations planted the seed of my life long interest in History, Religion, and Philosophy.

There are many people that I would like to especially thank because I recall our conversations more, but no one named in this book can be considered to have contributed more ideas than any other. In fact, it is very possible that strangers I spoke to helped guide me the most. With that in mind let me highlight several people. James and Kerry Gracia helped by discussing ideas and editing the original manuscript. James and I had a spoken word project when I started the book and we bounced many ideas off of each other. Ruben Remulla spoke with me at length about many things and he also opened his library to me and introduced me to some of our favorite historians. Abdul Hamza, Ed Konowicz, and Justin Miller are a few who took the time to discuss philosophy, science, and religion with me on many levels and parlayed some of their wisdom. I originally invited some people to write a chapter for this book but in retrospect it is good no one accepted my offer because that we all have a slightly different vision of the ideal book.

There are many people who also deserve a special mention and a few are; Doug Loucka, Nelson Loucka, Eric Johnston, Chris Johnston (who named me idle), Mike and Gretchen Martin, Judy Williams, Tom Galloway, Todd Robinette, Nancy Durant, Mike Gangloff, Larry May and Ashley, Nich Wheeley and Laura Ireland, Dean Rispler, Mathew Odietus and Jennifer Mcspadden, Sergio and Christa Ponce, Willy Johns, Anne Zuidema, Stewart Stansburry, Chris and Jen Walker Howe, Billy England, David and Holly Dennis, Kate Grottenthaller, Stacy Denny, Melissa Johnson, Michael "Blee" and Brenna Dennis, Jerry Henry, Chris and Kerry Nagle, Judy Williams, Eric Bryant, Myndi and Mike Selnore, Jamie and Stefan Parylak, Chris Medina and his brother, Ivan Stang. These are just a few of the people I have had many interesting conversations with and there are more in the friends edition.

There is a Friends edition of this book. This edition includes a more complete listing of my personal influences. I am so grateful to anyone who ever communicated with me on any level and I cannot express how important they all are. For every person listed, ten would be missed. For this reason, I would like to include the family members, significant others, and friends of those listed.

All places where people congregate forms a collective conscience and I appreciate tapping into the whole that we all are part of. I thank all the others who brought out ideas through conversation or writing. Ivan Stang, Emma Goldman, Michael Hoy, Carl Jaspers and all the great thinkers and writers that have inspired me along the way. I am grateful for the inspiration and writings of all Philosophers, Artists, Theologians, Bishops, Priests, Brahmin, Clerics, Imams, Those who spread the word of God from any religion, and all places of worship.

Special thanks and appreciation go out to reviewers of this book. They provided advice and suggestions that were important in the development of this book. White, Cindy Beals, Joe Faulkner, Alex Harrison, Dr. Kerry Hofheimer, and Dr. Chad Farries also helped me edit this book. If you saw the manuscript they were given you would know how much they have helped improve this book.

People who worked on the cover art for the first edition are very much appreciated. The artwork from the original chapbook is the cover of the first edition. I asked my sister Tamara to do the line drawing, I did the weapons, and Our sister Denise fixed the muscles and things. Jerry White revisited the drawing fifteen years later and did further touch ups. Finally, Jerry did the coloring, background and layout for the cover. My brother in law Christopher Davidson is an art consultant on this Book as are others family members and friends.

I would like to thank all the people who helped bring the lost books to the surface. Gratitude is owed to all. Historians of Religion. Some of the historians I used extensively in my research are Elain Pagels, Bart D. Ehrman, Hans Jonas, and Karen L. King. All people who helped translate and preserve the Nag Hammadi Codices, Dead Sea Scrolls, Jung Codex, Pistis Sophia Manuscripts and other ancient text.

To my nieces and nephews I am passing on the hope that they will revise this living testament and ensure continued publication of all editions. My hope is that they would do it together if possible. I would like to thank my siblings children in advance for considering my requested favor that within the next Forty or so years, they see to it that this book is revised by inserting enhancements, updates, completeness, and whatever they think will make it a better book including changing statements and adding to the literary effect. If not I would hope they promote this book and help ensure that it is in publication for eternity.

The people who have given me encouragement and support are to numerous to mention. If I mention one hundred I would miss one thousand. I love all the people I know and consider all of them friends even if we only looked at each other at a pub. People at shows, I love all the people in bands I have seen and all the people at school, work and places I go to. I want to thank those who support this book. I am grateful for the Stores and libraries that carry this book on their shelves. The clubs, Bands I have met or played with, All Spiritual leaders and those who help spread the word of God, Fathers, Mothers, Teachers, Students, Anarchists, Homeless people, and those who are reading this. Love goes out to all people including the unborn. Those who help promote the book. The appreciation I have for you the reader of this book can never be fully expressed in words. And finally, I would like to thank the lord Jesus himself for the inspiration which guided me in researching and writing this book.

POSTFACE

The Bible tells about his ministry and includes some of his teachings and methods that were ahead of their time, but it omits certain aspects such as reincarnation, equal rights for all regardless of sex, age, race, or religion. His original teachings included Judeo-Buddhist-Hindu aspects as well as some new ideas such as treating women, other races, the poor, the young and those with different sexual orientations equally. It also leaves out how he told his disciples to be willing to martyr themselves as proof of their faith in him and his resurrection.

Some argue that the four books that made it into the bible may not have even been dictated by John, Mark, Mathew, and Luke. John was an Essean and Simon Peter questioned his leadership. John the Baptist was Essean also and is not the disciple John. The last gospel of the Bible was written ninety years after the death of Jesus and was written anomalously. It is natural that they imparted their own influence into the words they claimed are from Jesus.

When the beginning of chapter one came out as a chap book called *Christ: The Dark Years* in 1992, it was released under a pseudonym. There was no History Channel etc. and people warned that the author may be silenced before the book got into the hands of the masses. The Author was part of a spoken word duo called The Church of New Faith and this was his moniker. In 2000 the Author began the task of completing this book. Many things in the original manuscript are not included and the vision of the book was changed as well. This book was always meant for people of any belief or non-belief system and is meant to complete the narrative given in the New and Old Testament

The book was started with two goals in mind. One was to complete the narrative on the life of Jesus, and the other to do it in a way that entertains atheists, believers, and agnostics alike. And while enjoying the story in its unique delivery, they all unwittingly come to love Jesus. Many have said that at first they didn't even know or believe anything about the bible before they heard our word. People have been saved and didn't even realize it until it was too late to turn back to their lost selves. The purpose of this book is to bring people closer to God and to guide them on the Journey of coming to know Christ. For the Bible asks for fishers of men and if this book is one of the hooks used, then its purpose has been fulfilled.

This book can be used as a reference book for the serious Bible group in deciding what guiding principles and beliefs they want to embrace. On the other hand, there is a small amount of historical conjecture in this book, and the presentation makes it so that not every detail lacks satire. With that being said, the release of this book reveals some deep and guarded secrets of some very powerful entities, so there are many forces at work trying to stop its publication. For this reason, each copy should be stored in an inconspicuous location and passed down to the next generation once they have gained the appropriate maturity and level of understanding.

The sequel, *The Secret Teachings of Jesus*, focuses on the resurrection of Jesus which is the most revolutionary thing about the rise of Christianity. The secrets Jesus shared with his inner circle of disciples and how they became the leaders of his Church are also revealed more deeply in *The Secret Teachings of Jesus*. For now the Author appreciates anyone who opens this book under any context.

www.ingramcontent.com/pod-product-compliance
Lightning Source LLC
Chambersburg PA
CBHW032008040426
42448CB00006B/538